A Still Forest Pool

Achaan Chah

A Still Forest Pool

The Insight Meditation of ACHAAN CHAH

Compiled & Edited by Jack Kornfield & Paul Breiter

This publication made possible with the assistance of the Kern Foundation

The Theosophical Publishing House
Wheaton, Ill. U.S.A.
Madras, India / London, England

The Theosophical Publishing House
306 West Geneva Road
Wheaton, Illinois 60187

A publication of the Theosophical Publishing House,
a department of the Theosophical Society in America.

Library of Congress Cataloging in Publication Data

Chah, Achaan.
  A still forest pool

    1. Spiritual life (Buddhism)   I. Sunno, Bhikkhu,
1945-   II. Breiter, Paul.   III. Title.
BQ5650.C45   1985   294.3'444   85-40411
ISBN 0-8356-0597-3 (pbk.)

Printed in the United States of America

Dedicated with deepest gratitude to the Venerable Achaan Chah Subato, our teacher, guide, and friend, to his many devoted students and disciples, especially Achaan Sumedho, to his teachers Achaan Tong Rath and Achaan Mun, and to the teachers before them, the lineage of centuries of those in the forest who realized through their simplicity and genuine practice the freedom and joy in the teachings of the Buddha. And dedicated to our parents, for their care and support along our way.

Try to be mindful, and let things take their natural course. Then your mind will become still in any surroundings, like a clear forest pool. All kinds of wonderful, rare animals will come to drink at the pool, and you will clearly see the nature of all things. You will see many strange and wonderful things come and go, but you will be still. This is the happiness of the Buddha.

Achaan Chah

Contents

Acknowledgments

We wish to thank and acknowledge assistance from many friends and teachers, especially the Venerable Achaan Sumedho (currently abbot of the forest wat at Chithurst, England) and the Venerable Pabakaro Bhikkhu the bhikkhu sangha at Wat Ba Na Na Chat, in Ubol Thailand, who reviewed and offered suggestions for this manuscript; Andy Taido Cooper and Steve Ikko Bodian of the Zen Center of Los Angeles; and especially to Shirley Nicholson and the Theosophical Publishing House for their valuable support and editorial assistance.

Portions of "Questions for the Teacher" and "Glossary of Buddhist Terms" are from *Living Buddhist Masters* by Jack Kornfield © 1977 and are reprinted by permission from Prajna Press, an imprint of Shambhala Publications, P.O. Box 308, Back Bay Annex, Boston, Mass., 02117. "A Monk's Life" and "Not Self" are from the film *The Mindful Way*, produced and broadcast by the British Broadcasting Corp., London, England, and are used by permission.

Foreword

It is a pleasure to write this foreword to the book of my Dharma friend, Achaan Chah.

Our world is at a very interesting age. In the West, people are studying yoga, karate, meditation—Eastern things. In the East, people are studying science, business, Western art and philosophy—Western things. This is now the time when Yin and Yang are changing very quickly. So if you are holding on to any idea—of what is Eastern, what is Western, how things are, how things ought to be—holding any idea, any opinion at all, then you will have a problem; you cannot connect with this world. But, if you lay it all down, all your ideas, all opinions, then the truth is right in front of your eyes: the sky is blue, the tree is green, sugar is sweet, salt is salty. The dog is barking, woof! woof! The rooster is crowing, cockle-doodle-doo! Then, when you're hungry, just eating, when you're tired, just sleeping is possible. A hungry person comes, you can give him food. A thirsty person comes, you can give him something to drink. That's all! That's enough! That is Buddhism—nothing at all.

Achaan Chah says, "People are like buffalo—unless they are tied down firmly by all four legs, they will not allow themselves to be given any medicine....In the same way, most of us must be totally bound up in suffering before we will let go and give up our delusions. If we can still writhe away, we will not yet give in. A few people can understand the Dharma when they hear it taught and explained by a teacher. But life must teach most of us all the way to the end." That is very wonderful speech, just correct!

Achaan Chah once walked by some students at the Insight Meditation Center who were doing slow walking meditation on the lawns. He remarked that the meditation center looked like a mental hospital for the diseases of the worldly mind. All afternoon, as he wandered past students, he would call out to them, "Get well soon. I hope you get well soon." That is also very wonderful.

He says, "Hey, listen. There's no one here, just this. No owner, no one to be old, to be young, to be good or bad, weak or strong....No one born and no one to die....When we carry a burden, it's heavy. When there's no one to carry it, there's not a problem in the world." That is the True Way.

Achaan Chah tells one good Zen story. "In the Zen koan of the flag in the wind, two persons are watching a flag: one says it is the wind that moves, the other says it is the flag. They can argue forever, take sticks and fight it out, all to no avail. It is the mind that moves." That is correct. But very important, if there is no mind, then no problem. If you have mind, you have a problem. So where does mind come from? Who made that?

Great Master Achaan Chah has already given you the Great Way, Truth and Correct Life. I hope you find your true way from this book, get Enlightenment, save all beings from suffering.

ZEN MASTER SEUNG SAHN
Providence Zen Center

Introduction

Suppose you were to go to Asia in the 1980s in search of living teachings of the Buddha, to discover if there are still monks and nuns practicing a life of simplicity and meditation, supported by alms-food, and dwelling in the forest. Perhaps you had read descriptions of the Buddha himself wandering with his monks in the forests of India, inviting men and women of good families to join him in cultivating wisdom and universal compassion, inviting them to live the simple life of a mendicant, to dedicate themselves to inner calm and awareness. Would you find this way of life alive today, twenty-five centuries later? And would its teachings still be applicable and relevant for our modern society, our modern minds?

You would land at a modern airport near Bangkok or Colombo or Rangoon. In your taxi you would drive through Asian city streets, passing cars, crowded busses, sidewalk vendors of tropical fruits. Every few blocks you would see the golden pagoda or spire of an urban Buddhist temple. But these are not the temples you have come to search for. They contain monks and nuns who study the ancient texts, who can chant and preach, and from this they teach. But to find the simple life of dwelling in the forest, the meditative living with robe and bowl, as old as the Buddha himself, you would have to leave the cities and their temples far behind. If it were Thailand, the country with the greatest number of monasteries and monks, you would board the train at busy Hualampong station, leaving early in the morning for the provinces of the far south or northeast.

The first hour's journey would take you clear of the urban sprawl, beyond the houses, businesses, and shanties backed up along the railway track. Vast plains of central Thailand would roll by, the green rice bowl of Southeast Asia. Mile after mile of paddy fields, checkerboarded into lots by small dikes between fields and rhythmically divided by canals and waterways. On the horizon of this sea of rice, every few miles in four or five directions you would see islands—dense clusters of palm and banana trees. If your train rolled close enough to one of these palm islands, you would see the glint of an orange-roofed monastery and cluster of wooden houses on stilts that make up a Southeast Asian village.

Every settled village, whether with five hundred or two thousand residents, has at least one monastery. It serves as the place for prayer, for ceremony, as the meeting hall, and for many years also served as the village school. Here is the place where most young men of the village will ordain at age twenty, for one year or three months, to learn enough of the ways of the Buddha to "ripen" into mature members of their society. The monastery is probably run by a few older, simple, and well-meaning monks who have studied some of the classic texts and know enough of ceremonies and of the basic teachings to serve as village priests. This monastery is an integral and beautiful part of village life, but it is not the temple you have come to search for.

Your train heads north toward the ancient capitol

of Auddhaya, filled with the ruins of magnificent temples and broken palaces that were sacked centuries ago in the periodic wars with neighboring kingdoms. The spirit of these magnificent ruins remains in the enormous stone Buddhas, imperturbably weathering the centuries.

Now your train turns east for the long journey toward the Lao border, across the reaches of the Korat Plateau. Hour after hour the land passes. Still you see rice paddies and villages, but they gradually become sparser and poorer. The canals and lush gardens of Central Thai villages, mango trees, and tropical greenery turn into a simpler landscape. Houses are smaller. Village monasteries still gleam, but they too are smaller and simpler. Here an older, more self-sufficient way of life is preserved. You can see women weaving handloomed blankets on their porches, while rice farmers work and children tend the water buffalo in wet gullies alongside the railroad tracks.

The rural countryside in these lesser developed provinces holds much of what remains of the tradition of forest monks and nuns. It still has regions of forest and jungle, small thickly covered mountains, and unsettled borderlands. And for many centuries it has supported forest monks and monasteries dedicated to the preservation and realization of the enlightenment of the Buddha. For the most part these monks do not function as village priests, nor do they teach school, nor study and preserve the language of the ancient written scriptures. Their intent is to live fully and realize in their own hearts and minds the insight and inner peace taught by the Buddha.

If you left the train and made your way by bus or hired car down some dirt road to such a monastery, one of dozens in northeast Thailand, what would you find? Would the teachings and way of practice be relevant in the 1980s? Would the insight and awareness training address the needs of one coming from a modern and complex society?

You would discover that many Westerners had come before you. Since 1965 hundreds of Europeans and Americans like you have come to visit and learn in the forest. Some came to study for short periods and then returned home to integrate what they learned into their household life. Some came to train more thoroughly as monks for one, two, or more years and then return home. Another group found life in the forest to be a rich and compelling way to live, and these remain in monasteries to this day.

For each of these groups the teachings have spoken directly to their hearts and minds, offering them a wise and conscious way to live. At first the way may seem almost easy, deceptively simple. But upon attempting to put the Buddha's way into practice, one discovers that it is not so easy. Yet, despite the effort it takes, these people feel that nothing could be more valuable than to discover the Dharma* or truth in one's own life.

From the moment of your entry into a forest monastery like Wat Ba Pong, the spirit of practice is evident. There is the stillness of trees rustling and the quiet movement of monks doing chores or mindful walking meditation. The whole monastery is spread over a hundred acres, divided into two sections for monks and nuns. The simple unadorned cottages are individually nestled in small forest clearings so that

---

*Dharma is a Buddhist expression which connotes the Buddha's teachings about universal law, its workings, and how it relates to us. See the Glossary for an explanation of Buddhist terms.

there are trees and silent paths between them. In the central area of the Wat are the main teaching hall, dining area, and chapel for ordination. The whole forest setting supports the atmosphere of simplicity and renunciation. You feel that you have finally arrived.

The monks who live in those monasteries have chosen to follow this uncomplicated and disciplined way of practice called *dhudanga*. The tradition of forest monks who voluntarily choose to follow a more austere way of life dates back to the Buddha, who allowed a supplementary code of thirteen special precepts, limiting the robes, food, and dwellings of monks. At the heart of this life style are few possessions, much meditation, and a once-daily round of alms-food begging. This way of life spread with the rest of Buddhism into the thick forests of Burma, Thailand, and Laos, places filled with caves and wild terrain, ideal for such intensive practice. These ascetic monks have traditionally been wanderers, living singly or in small groups, moving from one rural area to another, and using handmade cloth umbrella tents hung from trees as their temporary abode. Practical Dharma teachings from one of the greatest forest monasteries, Wat Ba Pong, and its master Achaan Chah have been translated and compiled and are offered to the West in this book.

Achaan Chah and his teachers, Achaan Tong Rath and Achaan Mun, themselves spent many years walking and meditating in these forests to develop their practice. From them and other forest teachers has come a legacy of immediate and powerful Dharma teachings, directed not toward ritual Buddhism or scholastic learning, but toward those who wish to purify their hearts and vision by actually living the teachings of the Buddha.

As great masters emerged in this forest tradition, laypersons and monks sought them out for teaching advice. Often, to make themselves available, these teachers would stop wandering and settle in a particular forest area where a *dhudanga* monastery would grow up around them. As population pressures have increased in this century, fewer forest areas are left for wanderers, and these forest monastery preserves of past and current masters are becoming the dwelling place of most ascetic and practice-oriented monks.

Wat Ba Pong monastery developed when Achaan Chah, after years of travel and meditation study, returned to settle in a thick forest grove near the village of his birth. The grove, uninhabited by humans, was known as a place of cobras, tigers, and ghosts—the perfect location for a forest monk, according to Achaan Chah. Around him a large monastery grew up.

From its beginnings as a few thatched huts in the forest, Wat Ba Pong has developed into one of the largest and best-run monasteries in Thailand. As Achaan Chah's skill and fame as a teacher have become widespread, the number of visitors and devotees has rapidly increased. In response to requests from devotees throughout Thailand, over fifty branch monasteries under the guidance of abbots trained by Achaan Chah have also been opened, including one near Wat Ba Pong especially designed for the many Western students who have come to seek Achaan Chah's guidance in the teachings. In recent years several branch monasteries and associated centers have been opened in Western countries as well, most notably the large forest Wat at Chithurst, England, run by Abbot Sumedho, Achaan Chah's Senior Western disciple.

Achaan Chah's teachings contain what has been called "the heart of Buddhist meditation," the direct and simple practices of calming the heart and opening the mind to true insight. This way of mindfulness or insight meditation has become a rapidly growing form of Buddhist practice in the West. Taught by monks and laypeople who have themselves studied in forest monasteries or intensive retreat centers, it provides a universal and direct way of training our bodies, our hearts, and our minds. It can teach us how to deal with greed and fear and sorrow and how to learn a path of patience, wisdom, and selfless compassion. This book is meant to provide guidance and counsel for those who wish to practice.

Achaan Chah's own practice started early in life and developed through years of wandering and austerity under the guidance of several great forest masters. He laughingly recalls how, even as a child, he wanted to play monk when the other children played house and would come to them with a make-believe begging bowl asking for candy and sweets. But his own practice was difficult, he relates, and the qualities of patience and endurance he developed are central to the teachings he gives his own disciples. A great inspiration for Achaan Chah as a young monk came from sitting at his father's sickbed during the last days and weeks of his father's life, directly facing the fact of decay and death. "When we don't understand death," Achaan Chah teaches, "life can be very con-fusing."

Because of this experience, Achaan Chah was strongly motivated in his practice to discover the causes of our worldly suffering and the source of peace and freedom taught by the Buddha. By his own account, he held nothing back, giving up everything for the Dharma, the truth. He encountered much hardship and suffering, including doubts of all kinds as well as physical illness and pain. Yet he stayed in the forest and sat—sat and watched—and, even though there were days when he could do nothing but cry, he brought what he calls a quality of daring to his practice. Out of this daring eventually grew wisdom, a joyful spirit, and an uncanny ability to help others.

Given spontaneously in the Thai and Lao languages, the teachings in this book reflect this joyful spirit of practice. Their flavor is clearly monastic, oriented to the community of men who have renounced the household life to join Achaan Chah in the forest. Hence frequent reference is made to *he* rather than *he or she*, and the emphasis is on the monks (an active community of forest nuns also exists) rather than laypersons. Yet the quality of the Dharma expressed here is immediate and universal, appropriate to each of us. Achaan Chah addresses the basic human problems of greed, fear, hatred, and delusion, insisting that we become aware of these states and of the real suffering that they cause in our lives and in our world. This teaching, the Four Noble Truths, is the first given by the Buddha and describes suffering, its cause, and the path to its end.

See how attachment causes suffering, Achaan Chah declares over and over. Study it in your experience. See the ever-changing nature of sight, sound, perception, feeling, and thought. Understanding the impermanent, insecure, selfless nature of life is Achaan Chah's message to us, for only when we see and accept all three characteristics can we live in peace. The forest tradition works directly with our understanding of and our resistance to these truths, with our fears and anger and desires. Achaan Chah tells us to confront our defilements and to use the tools of renunciation, perseverance, and awareness to overcome them. He urges us to learn not to be lost in our moods and anxieties but to train ourselves instead to see clearly and directly the true nature of mind and the world.

Inspiration comes from Achaan Chah's clarity and joy and the directness of his ways of practice in the forest. To be around him awakens in one the spirit of inquiry, humor, wonderment, understanding, and a deep sense of inner peace. If these pages capture a bit of that spirit in their instructions and tales of the forest life and inspire you to further practice, then their purpose is well served.

So listen to Achaan Chah carefully and take him to heart, for he teaches practice, not theory, and human happiness and freedom are his concerns. In the early years when Wat Ba Pong was starting to attract many visitors, a series of signs was posted along the entry path. "You there, coming to visit," the first one said, "be quiet! We're trying to meditate." Another stated simply, "To practice Dharma and realize truth is the only thing of value in this life. Isn't it time to begin?" In this spirit, Achaan Chah speaks to us directly, inviting us to quiet our hearts and investigate the truth of life. Isn't it time that we begin?

PART I
Understanding the Buddha's Teachings

Achaan Chah asks us to begin our practice simply and directly with the understanding that the Buddha's truths of suffering and liberation can be seen and experienced right here, within' our own bodies, hearts, and minds. The eightfold path, he tells us, is not to be found in books or scriptures but can be discovered in the workings of our own sense perceptions, our eyes, ears, nose, tongue, body, and mind. To study these in an immediate and wakeful way and cultivate mindfulness is the path of insight prescribed by the Buddha. It has been kept alive and followed by those monks, nuns, and laypeople inspired to devote themselves to practice in the centuries since.*

Achaan Chah speaks as a contemporary living representative of this ancient teaching. His wisdom and mastery have not come through study or tradition but are born of his years of practice, his diligent effort to employ meditation to calm the heart and awaken the mind. His own practice was inspired and guided by the wisdom of several great forest masters a generation before him. And he invites us to follow their example and his.

Look at what makes up your world—the six senses, the processes of body and mind. These processes will become clear through examination and an ongoing training of attention. As you observe note how fleeting and impermanent are each of the sense objects which appear. You will see the conditioned tendency to grasp or to resist these changing objects. Here, teaches Achaan Chah, is the place to learn a new way, the path of balance, the Middle Path.

Achaan Chah urges us to work with our practice,

---

*Note: For an explanation of Buddhist terms please consult the Glossary.

2

not as an ideal, but in our everyday life situations. It is here that we develop strength to overcome our difficulties and a constancy and greatness of heart. It is here, he says, in each moment that we can step out of our struggle with life and find the inner meaning of right understanding and with it the peace of the Buddha.

The Simple Path

Traditionally the Eightfold Path is taught with eight steps such as Right Understanding, Right Speech, Right Concentration, and so forth. But the true Eightfold Path is within us—two eyes, two ears, two nostrils, a tongue, and a body. These eight doors are our entire Path and the mind is the one that walks on the Path. Know these doors, examine them, and all the dharmas will be revealed.

The heart of the path is so simple. No need for long explanations. Give up clinging to love and hate, just rest with things as they are. That is all I do in my own practice.

Do not try to become anything. Do not make yourself into anything. Do not be a meditator. Do not become enlightened. When you sit, let it be. When you walk, let it be. Grasp at nothing. Resist nothing.

Of course, there are dozens of meditation techniques to develop samadhi and many kinds of vipassana. But it all comes back to this—just let it all be. Step over here where it is cool, out of the battle.

Why not give it a try? Do you dare?

The Middle Way

The Buddha does not want us to follow the double path—desire and indulgence on the one hand and fear and aversion on the other. Just be aware of pleasure, he teaches. Anger, fear, dissatisfaction are not the path of the yogi but the path of worldly people. The tranquil person walks the Middle Path of right practice, leaving grasping on the left and fear and aversion on the right.

One who undertakes the path of practice must follow this Middle Way: "I will not take interest in pleasure or pain. I will lay them down." But, of course, it is hard at first. It is as though we are being kicked on both sides. Like a cowbell or a pendulum, we are knocked back and forth.

When Buddha preached his first sermon, he discoursed on these two extremes because this is where attachment lies. The desire for happiness kicks from one side; suffering and dissatisfaction kick from the other. These two are always besieging us. But when you walk the Middle Path, you put them both down.

Don't you see? If you follow these extremes, you will simply strike out when you are angry and grab for what attracts you, without the slightest patience or forbearance. How long can you go on being trapped in this way? Consider it: if you like something, you follow after it when liking arises, yet it is just drawing you on to seek suffering. This mind of desire is really clever. Where will it lead you next?

The Buddha teaches us to keep laying down the extremes. This is the path of right practice, the path leading out of birth and becoming. On this path, there is neither pleasure nor pain, neither good nor evil. Alas, the mass of humans filled with desiring just strive for pleasure and always bypass the middle, missing the Path of the Excellent One, the path of the seeker of truth. Attached to birth and becoming, happiness and suffering, good and evil, the one who does not travel this Middle Path cannot become a wise one, cannot find liberation. Our Path is straight, the path of tranquility and pure awareness, calmed of both elation and sorrow. If your heart is like this, you can stop asking other people for guidance.

You will see that when the heart/mind is unattached, it is abiding in its normal state. When it stirs from the normal because of various thoughts and feelings, the process of thought construction takes place, in which illusions are created. Learn to see through this process. When the mind has stirred from normal, it leads away from right practice to one of the extremes of indulgence or aversion, thereby creating more illusion, more thought construction. Good or bad only arises in your mind. If you keep a watch on your mind, studying this one topic your whole life, I guarantee that you will never be bored.

Ending Doubt

Many people who have studied on a university level and attained graduate degrees and worldly success find that their lives are still lacking. Though they think high thoughts and are intellectually sophisticated, their hearts are still filled with pettiness and doubt. The vulture flies high, but what does it feed on?

Dharma is understanding that goes beyond the conditioned, compounded, limited understanding of worldly science. Of course, worldly wisdom can be used to good purpose, but progress in worldly wisdom can cause deterioration in religion and moral values. The important thing is to develop supermundane wisdom that can use such technology while remaining detached from it.

It is necessary to teach the basics first—basic morality, seeing the transitoriness of life, the facts of aging and death. Here is where we must begin. Before you drive a car or ride a bicycle, you must learn to walk. Later, you may ride in an airplane or travel around the world in the blink of an eye.

Outward, scriptural study is not important. Of course, the Dharma books are correct, but they are not right. They cannot give you right understanding. To see the word *hatred* in print is not the same as experiencing anger, just as hearing a person's name is

8

different from meeting him. Only experiencing for yourself can give you true faith.

There are two kinds of faith. One is a kind of blind trust in the Buddha, the teachings, the master, which often leads one to begin practice or to ordain. The second is true faith—certain, unshakable—which arises from knowing within oneself. Though one still has other defilements to overcome, seeing clearly all things within oneself makes it possible to put an end to doubt, to attain this certainty in one's practice.

Go Beyond Words: See for Yourself

In my own practice, I did not know or study much. I took the straightforward teachings the Buddha gave and simply began to study my own mind according to nature. When you practice, observe yourself. Then gradually knowledge and vision will arise of themselves. If you sit in meditation and want it to be this way or that, you had better stop right there. Do not bring ideals or expectations to your practice. Take your studies, your opinions, and store them away.

You must go beyond all words, all symbols, all plans for your practice. Then you can see for yourself the truth, arising right here. If you do not turn inward, you will never know reality. I took the first few years of formal Dharma text study, and when I had the opportunity, I went to hear various scholars and masters teach, until such study became more of a hindrance than a help. I did not know how to listen to their sermons because I had not looked within.

The great meditation masters spoke about the truth within oneself. Practicing, I began to realize that it existed in my own mind as well. After a long time, I realized that these teachers have really seen the truth and that if we follow their path, we will encounter everything they have spoken about. Then we will be able to say, "Yes, they were right. What else could there be? Just this." When I practiced diligently, realization unfolded like that.

If you are interested in Dharma, just give up, just let go. Merely thinking about practice is like pouncing on the shadow and missing the substance. You need not study much. If you follow the basics and practice accordingly, you will see the Dharma for yourself. There must be more than merely hearing the words. Speak just with yourself, observe your own mind. If you cut off this verbal, thinking mind, you will have a true standard for judging. Otherwise, your understanding will not penetrate deeply. Practice in this way and the rest will follow.

Buddhist Psychology

One day, a famous woman lecturer on Buddhist metaphysics came to see Achaan Chah. This woman gave periodic teachings in Bangkok on the abhidharma and complex Buddhist psychology. In talking to Achaan Chah, she detailed how important it was for people to understand Buddhist psychology and how much her students benefited from their study with her. She asked him whether he agreed with the importance of such understanding.

"Yes, very important", he agreed.

Delighted, she further questioned whether he had his own students learn abhidharma.

"Oh, yes, of course."

And where, she asked, did he recommend they start, which books and studies were best?

"Only here," he said, pointing to his heart, "only here."

Study and Experiencing

Let us talk about the difference between studying
Dharma ideas and applying them in practice. True
Dharma study has only one purpose—to find a way
out of the unsatisfactoriness of our lives and to
achieve happiness and peace for ourselves and all beings. Our suffering has causes for its arising and a
place to abide. Let us understand this process. When
the heart is still, it is in its normal condition; when
the mind moves, thought is constructed. Happiness
and sorrow are part of this movement of mind, this
thought construction. So also is restlessness, the desire
to go here and there. If you do not understand such
movement, you will chase after thought constructions
and be at their mercy.

Therefore, the Buddha taught us to contemplate the
movements of the mind. Watching the mind move, we
can see its basic characteristics: endless flux, unsatisfactoriness, and emptiness. You should be aware of
and contemplate these mental phenomena. In this
way, you can learn about the process of dependent
origination. The Buddha taught that ignorance is the
cause of the arising of all worldly phenomena and of
our volitions. Volition gives rise to consciousness, and
consciousness in turn gives rise to mind and body.
This is the process of dependent origination.

When we first study Buddhism, these traditional

13

teachings may appear to make sense to us. But when the process is actually occurring within us, those who have only read about it cannot follow fast enough. Like a fruit falling from a tree, each link in the chain falls so fast that such people cannot tell what branches it has passed. When pleasurable sense contact takes place, for example, they are carried away by the sensation and are unable to notice how it happened.

Of course, the systematic outline of the process in the texts is accurate, but the experience is beyond textual study. Study does not tell you that *this* is the experience of ignorance arising, *this* is how volition feels, *this* is a particular kind of consciousness, *this* is the feeling of the different elements of body and mind. When you let go of a tree limb and fall to the ground, you do not go into detail about how many feet and inches you fell; you just hit the ground and experience the pain. No book can describe that.

Formal Dharma study is systematic and refined, but reality does not follow a single track. Therefore, we must attest to what arises from the one who knows, from our deepest wisdom. When our innate wisdom, the one who knows, experiences the truth of the heart / mind, it will be clear that the mind is not our self. Not belonging to us, not I, not mine, all of it must be dropped. As to our learning the names of all the elements of mind and consciousness, the Buddha did not want us to become attached to the words. He just wanted us to see that all this is impermanent, unsatisfactory, and empty of self. He taught only to let go. When these things arise, be aware of them, know them. Only a mind that can do this is properly trained.

When the mind is stirred up, the various mental formations, thought constructions, and reactions start arising from it, building and proliferating continually. Just let them be, the good as well as the bad. The Buddha said simply, "Give them up." But for us, it is necessary to study our own minds to know how it is possible to give them up.

If we look at the model of the elements of mind, we see that it follows a natural sequence: mental factors are thus, consciousness arises and passes like this, and so forth. We can see in our own practice that when we have right understanding and awareness, then right thought, right speech, right action, and right livelihood automatically follow. Different mental elements arise from that very one who knows. The one who knows is like a lamp. If understanding is right, thought and all the other factors will be right as well, like the light emanating from the lamp. As we watch with awareness, right understanding grows.

When we examine all that we call mind, we see only a conglomeration of mental elements, not a self. Then where can we stand? Feeling, memory, all the five aggregates of mind and body are shifting like leaves in the wind. We can discover this through meditation.

Meditation is like a single log of wood. Insight and investigation are one end of the log; calm and concentration are the other end. If you lift up the whole log, both sides come up at once. Which is concentration and which is insight? Just this mind.

You cannot really separate concentration, inner tranquility, and insight. They are just as a mango that is first green and sour, then yellow and sweet, but not two different fruits. One grows into the other; without the first, we would never have the second. Such terms are only conventions for teaching. We should not be attached to the language. The only source of true knowledge is to see what is within ourself. Only this kind of study has an end and is the study of real value.

The calmness of the mind at the beginning stage of concentration arises from the simple practice of one-pointedness. But when this calm departs, we suffer because we have become attached to it. The attainment of tranquillity is not yet the end, according to the Buddha. Becoming and suffering still exist.

Thus, the Buddha took this concentration, this tranquillity, and contemplated further. He searched out the truth of the matter until he was no longer attached to tranquillity. Tranquillity is just another relative reality, one of numerous mental formations, only a stage on the path. If you are attached to it, you will find yourself still stuck in birth and becoming, based on your pleasure in tranquillity. When tranquillity ceases, agitation will begin and you will be attached even more.

The Buddha went on to examine becoming and birth to see where they arise. As he did not yet know the truth of the matter, he used his mind to contemplate further, to investigate all the mental elements that arose. Whether tranquil or not, he continued to penetrate, to examine further, until he finally realized that all that he saw, all the five aggregates of body and mind, were like a red-hot iron ball. When it is red-hot all over, where can you find a cool spot to touch? The same is true of the five aggregates—to grasp any part causes pain. Therefore, you should not get attached even to tranquillity or concentration; you should not say that peace or tranquillity is you or yours. To do so just creates the painful illusion of self, the world of attachment and delusion, another red-hot iron ball.

In our practice, our tendency is to grasp, to take experiences as me and mine. If you think, "I am calm, I am agitated, I am good or bad, I am happy or unhappy," this clinging causes more becoming and birth. When happiness ends, suffering appears; when suffering ends, happiness appears. You will see yourself unceasingly vacillating between heaven and hell. The Buddha saw that the condition of his mind was thus, and he knew, because of this birth and becoming, his liberation was not yet complete. So he took up these elements of experience and contemplated their true nature. Because of grasping, birth and death exist. Becoming glad is birth; becoming dejected is death. Having died, we are then born; having been born, we die. This birth and death from one moment to the next is like the endless spinning of a wheel.

The Buddha saw that whatever the mind gives rise to are just transitory, conditioned phenomena, which are really empty. When this dawned on him, he let go, gave up, and found an end to suffering. You too must understand these matters according to the truth. When you know things as they are, you will see that these elements of mind are a deception, in keeping with the Buddha's teaching that this mind has nothing, does not arise, is not born, and does not die with anyone. It is free, shining, resplendent, with nothing to occupy it. The mind becomes occupied only because it misunderstands and is deluded by these conditioned phenomena, this false sense of self.

Therefore, the Buddha had us look at our minds. What exists in the beginning? Truly, not anything. This emptiness does not arise and die with phenomena. When it contacts something good, it does not become good; when it contacts something bad, it does not become bad. The pure mind knows these objects clearly, knows that they are not substantial.

When the mind of the meditator abides like this, no doubt exists. Is there becoming? Is there birth? We need not ask anyone. Having examined the elements of mind, the Buddha let them go and became merely one who was aware of them. He just watched with equanimity. Conditions leading to birth did not exist for him. With his complete knowledge, he called them all impermanent, unsatisfactory, empty of self. Therefore, he became the one who knows with certainty. The one who knows sees according to this truth and does not become happy or sad according to changing conditions. This is true peace, free of birth, aging, sickness, and death, not dependent on causes, results, or conditions, beyond happiness and suffering, above good and evil. Nothing can be spoken about it. No conditions promote it any longer.

Therefore, develop samadhi, calm and insight; learn to make them arise in your mind and really use them. Otherwise, you will know only the words of Buddhism and with the best intentions, go around merely describing the characteristics of existence. You may be clever, but when things arise in your mind, will you follow them? When you come into contact with something you like, will you immediately become attached? Can you let go of it? When unpleasant experiences arise, does the one who knows hold that dislike in his mind, or does he let go? If you see things that you dislike and still hold on to or condemn them, you should reconsider—this is not yet correct, not yet the supreme. If you observe your mind in this way, you will truly know for yourself.

I did not practice using textbook terms; I just looked at this one who knows. If it hates someone, ques-

18

tion why. If it loves someone, question why. Probing all arising back to its origin, you can solve the problem of clinging and hating and get them to leave you alone. Everything comes back to and arises from the one who knows. But repeated practice is crucial.

The Chicken or the Egg?

During his first visit to England, Achaan Chah spoke
to many Buddhist groups. One evening after a talk he
received a question from a dignified English lady who
had spent many years studying the complex cyber-
netics of the mind according to the eighty-nine
classes of consciousness in the Buddhist abhidharma
psychology texts. Would he please explain certain of
the more difficult aspects of this system of psychology
to her so she could continue her study?

Dharma teaches us to let go. But at first, we
naturally cling to the principles of Dharma. The wise
person takes these principles and uses them as tools to
discover the essence of our life.

Sensing how caught up she was in intellectual concepts rather than benefiting from practice in her own
heart, Achaan Chah answered her quite directly,
"You, madam, are like one who keeps hens in her
yard," he told her, "and goes around picking up the
chicken droppings instead of the eggs."

Thieves in Your Heart

The purpose of meditation is to raise things up and put them to the test, to understand their essence. For example, we see the body as something fine and beautiful, whereas the Buddha tells us it is unclean, impermanent, and prone to suffering. Which view accords with the truth?

We are like visitors to a foreign country; not knowing the language, we cannot enjoy ourselves. But once we have learned the language, we can laugh and joke with others. Or we are like children who have to grow up before we can understand what the grown-ups are saying.

The normal view is that the elements of our life, beginning with the body, are stable. One child plays with his balloon until it catches on a branch or a thorn and bursts, leaving him in tears. Another child, smarter than the first, knows that his balloon can burst easily and is not upset when it does. People go through life blindly, ignoring the fact of death like gourmets feasting on fine foods, never thinking they will have to excrete. Then nature calls, but having made no provision, they do not know where to go.

There is danger in the world—danger from the elements, danger from thieves. These dangers have their counterpart in the temples too. The Buddha taught us to investigate these dangers and gave the name *bhikkhu* to one who ordains. *Bhikkhu* has two meanings: one who begs and one who sees danger in the round of samsara, of grasping. Beings experience greed, hatred, and delusion. Succumbing to these defilements, they reap the results, increase their bad habits, make yet more karma, and again succumb to defilements.

Why can't you get rid of greed, hatred, and delusion? If your thinking is wrong, you will suffer; if you understand correctly, you can end suffering.

Know the workings of karma, of cause and effect. Attachment to pleasure brings suffering in its wake. You gorge yourself on good food, but stomach trouble and intestinal discomfort follow. Or you steal something and are happy with it, but later the police come around to arrest you. When you watch, you can learn how to act, you can learn to end grasping and sorrow. The Buddha, seeing this, wanted to escape from the real dangers of the world, which we have to overcome within ourselves. External dangers are not as frightening as the dangers within: What are the elements of this inner danger?

Wind. Things come at the senses, causing compulsion, lust, anger, and ignorance to arise, destroying what is good in us. Normally, we see the wind only as that which blows the leaves about, not seeing the wind of our senses, which, unwatched, can cause the storms of desire.

Fire. Our temple may never have been struck by fire, but greed, hatred, and delusion burn us constantly. Lust and aversion cause us to speak and do wrong; delusion leads us to see good as bad, bad as good, the ugly as beautiful, the valueless as valuable. But one who does not meditate does not see this and is overcome by these fires.

Water. Here the danger is the flood of defilement in our hearts submerging our true nature.

Thieves. The real thieves do not exist outside us. Our monastery has seen thieves only once in twenty years, but inwardly the five gangs of attachment, the aggregates, are ever robbing, beating, and destroying us. What are these five aggregates?

1. *Body.* It is a prey to illness and pain; when it does not accord with our wishes, we have grief and sorrow. Not understanding the natural aging and decay of the body, we suffer. We feel attraction or repulsion toward the bodies of others and are robbed of true peace.

2. *Feelings.* When pain and pleasure arise, we forget that they are impermanent, suffering, not self; we identify with our emotions and are thus tortured by our wrong understanding.

3. *Memories and perceptions.* Identifying with what we recognize and remember gives rise to greed, hatred, and delusion. Our wrong understanding becomes habitual, stored in the subconscious.

4. *Volitions and other elements of mind.* Not understanding the nature of mental states, we react, and thoughts and feelings, likes and dislikes, happiness and sorrow arise. Forgetting that they are impermanent, suffering, and selfless, we cling to them.

5. *Consciousness.* We grasp that which knows the other aggregates. We think, "I know, I am, I feel," and are bound by this illusion of self, of separation.

All these thieves, this wrong understanding, leads to

wrong action. The Buddha had no desire for this; he saw that there was no true happiness to be found here. Thus, he gave the name *bhikkhu* to those who also see this danger and seek a way out.

The Buddha taught his monks the true nature of the five aggregates and how to let go of them without clinging to them as me or mine. When we understand them, we will see that they have potential for great harm or great value, but they do not disappear. They are simply no longer grasped as our own. After his enlightenment, the Buddha still had physical ills, had feelings of pain and pleasure, had memories, thoughts, and consciousness. But he did not cling to them as being self, as being me or mine. He knew them as they were, and the one who knew was also not I, not self.

Separating the five aggregates from the defilements and from clinging is like clearing the brush in the forest without destroying the trees. There is just a constant arising and falling away; defilement cannot gain a foothold. We are simply being born and dying with the aggregates; they just come and go, according to their nature.

If someone curses us and we have no feelings of self, the incident ends with the spoken words, and we do not suffer. If unpleasant feelings arise, we should let them stop there, realizing that the feelings are not us. " He hates me, he troubles me, he is my enemy." A bhikkhu does not think like this, nor does he hold views of pride or comparison. If we do not stand up in the line of fire, we do not get shot; if there is no one to receive it, the letter is sent back. Moving gracefully through the world not caught in evaluating each event, a bikkhu becomes serene. This is the way of Nirvana, empty and free.

Investigate the five aggregates, then; make a clean forest. You will be a different person. Those who understand emptiness and practice accordingly are few, but they come to know the greatest joy. Why not try it? You can abolish the thieves in your heart and set everything right.

PART II
Correcting Our Views

When you pick mushrooms, Achaan Chah cautions, you must know what to look for. When you undertake spiritual practice you must also know what attitudes to nourish, what dangers to avoid, and what mental qualities to encourage.

Here he emphasizes the power of training our endurance and courage, developing a willingness to find the Middle Path and follow it despite temptation and defilement. When greed, hatred, or delusion arise, he says, don't give in to them. Don't be discouraged. Just stay mindful and strong in your resolve.

As your training develops you will see that every single experience you pass through is impermanent, and thus unsatisfactory. You will discover firsthand the endless truth of these characteristics in all existence and begin to learn the way of freedom, of nonattachment. But Achaan Chah reminds us that this requires a willingness to investigate both our sufferings and our joys with an equal mind.

When the heart becomes calm and the mind clear, we come closer to the truth of what Achaan Chah calls, "Just that much." The Dharma, the truth, is really very simple. All things that arise and pass, the whole world of changing phenomena, is really only "that much!" When we truly discover what this means, then here in our world we can come to peace.

The Wrong Road

A wandering ascetic, having heard of the Buddha, traveled everywhere looking for him. One night he came to stay in a house where the Buddha was also staying but, not knowing the Buddha's physical appearance, he was unaware of his presence. The next morning he arose and continued on his way, still searching for the Buddha. To search for peace and enlightenment without correct understanding is like this.

Due to a lack of understanding of the truth of suffering and its elimination, all the subsequent factors on the path will be wrong—wrong intentions, wrong speech, wrong actions, and wrong practice of concentration and tranquillity. Your likes and dislikes are not a trustworthy guide in this matter either, although foolish people may take them for their ultimate reference. Alas, it is like traveling to a certain town—you unknowingly start out on the wrong road, and since it is a convenient one, you travel it in comfort. But it will not take you where you want to go.

Right Understanding

One develops right understanding by seeing impermanence, suffering, and not-self in everything, which
leads to detachment and loss of infatuation. Detachment is not aversion. An aversion to something we
once liked is temporary, and the craving for it will
return.

Imagine some food that you like—bamboo shoots
or sweet curry, for example. Imagine having it everyday for five or six years; you would get tired of bamboo shoots. If someone were to offer you some, you
would not get excited. In the same way, we should see
impermanence, suffering, and emptiness in all things
at all times: bamboo shoots!

We seek not for a life of pleasure, but to find
peace. Peace is within oneself, to be found in the same
place as agitation and suffering. It is not found in a
forest or on a hilltop, nor is it given by a teacher.
Where you experience suffering, you can also find
freedom from suffering. To try to run away from suffering is actually to run toward it. Investigate suffering, see its causes, and put an end to them right now,
rather than merely dealing with their effects.

Starving Defilements

Those just beginning often wonder what practice is. Practice occurs when you try opposing the defilements, not feeding old habits. Where friction and difficulty arise, that's the place to work.

When you pick mushrooms to eat, you do not do so blindly; you have to know which kind is which. So too with our practice—we must know the dangers, the snake's bite of defilements, in order to free ourselves from them.

The defilements—greed, hatred and delusion—are at the root of our suffering and our selfishness. We must learn to overcome them, to conquer and go beyond their control, to become masters of our minds. Of course it seems hard. It is like having the Buddha tell you to split up with a friend you have known since childhood.

The defilements are like a tiger. We should imprison the tiger in a good strong cage made of mindfulness, energy, patience, and endurance. Then we can let it starve to death by not feeding its habitual desires. We do not have to take a knife and butcher it.

Or defilements are like a cat. If you feed it, it will keep coming around. Stop feeding it, and eventually it will not bother to come around any more.

We will unavoidably be hot and distressed in our practice at first. But remember, only the defilements are hot. People think, "I never had problems like this before. What's wrong?" Before, when we fed our desires, we were at peace with them, like a man who takes care of an internal infection by dressing only the external sores.

Resist defilements. Do not give them all the food or sleep they want. Many people consider this the extreme of self-torture, but it is necessary to become inwardly strong. See for yourself. Constantly watching the mind, you may think you are seeing only effects and wonder about the causes. Suppose parents have a child who grows up to be disrespectful. Distressed by his behavior, they may ask, "Where has this child come from?" Actually, our suffering comes from our own wrong understanding, our attachment to various mental activities. We must train our mind like a buffalo: the buffalo is our thinking, the owner is the meditator, raising and training the buffalo is the practice. With a trained mind, we can see the truth, we can know the cause of our self and its end, the end of all sorrow. It is not complicated, you know.

Everyone has defilements in his practice. We must work with them, struggling when they arise. This is not something to think about but to do. Much patience is necessary. Gradually we have to change our habitual ways of thinking and feeling. We must see how we suffer when we think in terms of *me* and *mine*. Then we can let go.

Happiness and Suffering

A young Western monk had just arrived at one of Achaan Chah's forest monasteries and asked permission to stay and practice.

"I hope you're not afraid of suffering" was Achaan Chah's first response.

Somewhat taken aback, the young Westerner explained that he did not come to suffer but to learn meditation and to live peacefully in the forest.

Achaan Chah explained, "There are two kinds of suffering: the suffering that leads to more suffering and the suffering that leads to the end of suffering. If you are not willing to face the second kind of suffering, you will surely continue to experience the first."

Achaan Chah's way of teaching is usually straightforward and direct. When he meets his monks on the monastery grounds, he often asks, "Are you suffering much today?" If one answers yes, he replies, "Well, you must have many attachments today," and then laughs with the monk about it.

Have you ever had happiness? Have you ever had suffering? Have you ever considered which of these is really valuable? If happiness is true, then it should not dissolve, should it? You should study this point to see what is real, what is true. This study, this meditation, leads to right understanding.

The Discriminating Mind

Right understanding ultimately means nondiscrimination—seeing all people as the same, neither good nor bad, neither clever nor foolish; not thinking that honey is sweet and good and some other food is bitter. Although you may eat several kinds of food, when you absorb and excrete them, they all become the same. Is it one or many? Is a glass big? In relation to a little cup, yes; when placed next to a pitcher, no.

Our desire and ignorance, our discrimination color everything in this way. This is the world we create. Again, a pitcher is neither heavy nor light; we just feel that it is one way or the other. In the Zen koan of the flag in the wind, two persons are watching a flag: one says it is the wind that moves, the other says it is the flag. They can argue forever, take sticks and fight it out, all to no avail, for it is the mind that moves.

There are always differences. Get to know those differences, yet learn to see the sameness too. In our group people come from different backgrounds, different cultures. Yet without thinking, "This one's Thai, that one's Lao, he's Cambodian, he's a Westerner," we should have mutual understanding and respect for the ways of others. Learn to see the underlying sameness of all things, how they are all truly equal, truly empty. Then you can know how to deal with the apparent differences wisely. But do not get attached even to this sameness.

Why is sugar sweet and water tasteless? It is just their nature. So too with thinking and stillness, pain and pleasure—it is wrong understanding to want thinking to cease. Sometimes there is thought, sometimes stillness. We must see that both are by nature impermanent, unsatisfactory, not a cause for lasting happiness. But if we continue to worry and think further, "I am suffering, I want to stop thinking," this wrong understanding only complicates things.

At times, we may feel that thinking is suffering, like a thief robbing us of the present. What can we do to stop it? In the day, it is light; at night, it is dark. Is this itself suffering? Only if we compare the way things are now with other situations we have known and wish it were otherwise. Ultimately things are just as they are—only our comparisons cause us to suffer.

You see this mind at work—do you consider it to be you or yours? "I don't know if it's me or mine," you answer, "but it's certainly out of control." It is just like a monkey jumping about senselessly. It goes upstairs, gets bored, runs back downstairs, gets tired of that, goes to a movie, gets bored again, has good food or poor food, gets bored with that too. Its behavior is driven not by dispassion but by different forms of aversion and fear.

You have to learn control. Stop caring for the monkey—care for the truth of life instead. See the real nature of the mind: impermanent, unsatisfactory, empty. Learn to be its master; chain it down if you must. Do not just follow it, let it wear itself out and die. Then you have a dead monkey. Let the dead monkey rot away, and you have monkey's bones.

Still enlightenment does not mean to become dead like a Buddha statue. One who is enlightened thinks also but knows the process as impermanent, unsatisfactory, and empty of self. We who practice must see these things clearly. We need to investigate suffering and stop its causes. If we do not see it, wisdom can never arise. There should be no guesswork, we must see things exactly as they are—feelings are just feelings, thoughts are just thoughts. This is the way to end all our problems.

We can see the mind as a lotus. Some lotuses are still stuck in the mud, some have climbed above the mud but are still underwater, some have reached the surface, while others are open in the sun, stain-free. Which lotus do you choose to be? If you find yourself below the surface, watch out for the bites of fishes and turtles.

Sense Objects and the Mind

We do not examine ourselves; we just follow desire, caught in endless rounds of grasping and fearing, wanting to do just as we please. Whatever we do, we want it to be at our ease. If we are not able to have comfort and pleasure any longer, we are unhappy, anger and aversion arise, and we suffer, trapped by our mind.

For the most part, our thinking follows sense objects, and, wherever thought leads us, we follow. However, thinking and wisdom are different; in wisdom, the mind becomes still, unmoving, and we are simply aware, simply acknowledging. Normally, when sense objects come, we think about, dwell on, discourse over, and worry about them. Yet none of those objects is substantial; all are impermanent, unsatisfactory, and empty. Just cut them short and dissect them into these three common characteristics. When you sit again, they will arise again, but just keep observing them, keep checking them out.

This practice is like caring for a buffalo and a rice field. The mind is like the buffalo that wants to eat the rice plants, sense objects; the one who knows is the owner. Consider the comparison. When you tend a buffalo, you let it go free but you keep watch over it. You cannot be heedless. If it goes close to the rice plants, you shout at it and it retreats. If it is stubborn and will not obey your voice, you take a stick and hit it. Do not fall asleep in the daytime and let everything go. If you do, you will have no rice plants left, for sure.

When you are observing your mind, the one who knows constantly notices all. As the sutras say, "He who watches over his mind shall escape the snares of Mara the Evil One." Mind is mind, but who is it that observes it? Mind is one thing, the one who knows is another. At the same time the mind is both the thinking process and the knowing. Know the mind—know how it is when it meets sense objects and how it is when it is apart from them. When the one who knows observes the mind in this way, wisdom arises. If it meets an object, it gets involved, just like the buffalo. Wherever it goes, you must watch it. When it goes near the rice plants, shout at it. If it will not obey, just give it the stick.

When the mind experiences sense contact, it grabs hold. When it grabs hold, the one who knows must teach it—explaining what is good and what is bad, pointing out the workings of cause and effect, showing that anything it holds on to will bring undesirable results—until mind becomes reasonable, until it lets go. In this way, the training will take effect, and the mind will become tranquil.

The Buddha taught us to lay everything down, not like a cow or a buffalo but knowingly, with awareness. In order for us to know, he taught us to practice much, develop much, rest firmly on the principles of the Buddha, Dharma, and Sangha, and apply them directly to our own life.

From the beginning I have practiced like this. In teaching my disciples, I teach like this. We want to see the truth not in a book or as an ideal but in our own minds. If the mind is not yet free, contemplate the cause and effect of each situation until the mind sees clearly and can free itself from its own conditioning. As the mind becomes attached again, examine each new situation—do not stop looking, keep at it, drive the point home. Then attachment will find nowhere to rest. This is the way I myself have practiced.

If you practice like this, true tranquillity is found in activity, in the midst of sense objects. At first, when you are working on your mind and sense objects come, you cling to them or avoid them. You are therefore disturbed, not peaceful. When you sit and wish not to have sense contact, not to have thinking the very wish not to have is desire. The more you struggle with your thinking, the stronger it becomes. Just forget about it and continue to practice. When you make contact with sense objects, contemplate: impermanent, unsatisfactory, not self. Throw everything into these three pigeonholes, file everything under these three categories, and keep contemplating.

Problems of the World

Many people, particularly educated, professional people, are moving out of the big cities, seeking quieter living and simpler livelihood in the small towns and rural areas. This is natural. If you grab a handful of mud and squeeze it, it will ooze through your fingers. People under pressure likewise seek a way out.

People ask me about the problems of our world, about a coming apocalypse. I ask, what does it mean to be worldly? What is the world? You do not know? This very unknowing, this very darkness, this very place of ignorance, is what is meant by worldly. Caught in the six senses, our knowledge develops as a part of this darkness. To come to an answer to the problems of the world, we must know its nature completely and realize the wisdom that shines above the darkness of the world.

These days, it seems that our culture is deteriorating, lost in greed, hatred, and delusion. But the culture of the Buddha never changes, never diminishes. It says, "Do not lie to others or to ourselves. Do not steal from others or from ourselves." Worldly culture has desire as its director and guide. The culture of the Buddha has compassion and Dharma, or truth, as its guide.

Just That Much

When you take a good look at it, this world of ours is just that much; it exists just as it is. Ruled by birth, aging, sickness, and death, it is only that much. Great or little is only that much. The wheel of life and death is only that much. Then why are we still attached, caught up, not removed? Playing around with the objects of life gives us some enjoyment; yet this enjoyment is also just that much.

Whatever is pleasurable, delicious, exciting, good, is just that much; it has its limit, it is not as if it is anything outstanding. The Buddha taught that everything is just that much, of equal value. We should contemplate this point. Just look at the Western monks who have come here to practice. They have experienced much pleasure and comfort in their lives, but it was only that much; trying to make more of it just drove them crazy. They became world travelers, let everything go—it was still only that much. Then they came here to the forest to learn to give it all up, all attachments, all suffering.

All conditioned things are the same—impermanent, caught up in the cycle of birth and death. Just look at them; they are only that much. All things in this world exist thus. Some people say, "Doing virtuous deeds, practicing religion, you grow old just the same." This may be true of the body, but not of the heart, of virtue; when we understand the difference, we have a chance to become free.

Look at the elements of our body and mind. They are conditioned phenomena, arising from a cause and therefore impermanent. Their nature is always the same, it cannot be changed. A great noble and a common servant are the same. When they become old, their act comes to an end; they can no longer put on airs or hide behind masks. There is nowhere to go, no more taste, no more texture. When you get old, your sight becomes dim, your hearing weakens, your body becomes feeble—you must face yourself.

We human beings are constantly in combat, at war to escape the fact of being just that much. But instead of escaping, we continue to create more suffering, waging war with good, waging war with evil, waging war with what is small, waging war with what is big, waging war with what is short or long or right or wrong, courageously carrying on the battle.

The Buddha taught the truth, but we are like buffalo—unless they are tied down firmly by all four legs, they will not allow themselves to be given any medicine. Once they have been tied down and cannot do anything—aha, now you can go ahead and give them medicine, and they are unable to struggle away. In the same way, most of us must be totally bound up in suffering before we will let go and give up our delusions. If we can still writhe away, we will not yet give in. A few people can understand the Dharma when they hear it taught and explained by a teacher. But life must teach most of us all the way to the end.

You can pull on the end of a rope, but if the other end is stuck, the rope will never budge. In order to make it come free, you need to find out where it is stuck, you need to seek out the source or the root of the problem. We must use our practice fully to discover how we are stuck, to discover the heart of peace. We must follow the ox's tracks from the beginning, from the point at which it left the corral. If we start in the middle of the trail, we will not be able to tell whose ox's tracks they are, and thus we could be led anywhere.

Therefore, the Buddha spoke of first correcting our views. We must investigate the very root of suffering, the very truth of our life. If we can see that all things are just that much, we will find the true Path. We must come to know the reality of conditioned phenomena, the way things are. Only then can we have peace in our world.

Follow Your Teacher

As you grow in Dharma, you should have a teacher to instruct and advise you. The matter of concentrating the mind, of samadhi, is much misunderstood; phenomena occur in meditation that otherwise do not normally arise. When this happens, a teacher's guidance is crucial, expecially in those areas in which you have wrong understanding. Often where he corrects you will be just where you thought you were right. In the complexity of your thinking, one view may obscure the other and you get fooled. Respect your teacher and follow the rules or system of practice. If the teacher says to do something, do it. If he says to desist, desist. This allows you to make an honest effort and leads to making knowledge and vision manifest in your mind. If you do as I am saying, you will see and know.

True teachers speak only of the difficult practice of giving up or getting rid of the self. Whatever may happen, do not abandon the teacher. Let him guide you, because it is easy to forget the Path.

Alas, few who study Buddhism really want to practice. I certainly urge them to practice, but some people can only study in a logical way. Few are willing to die and be born again free. I feel sorry for the rest.

Trust Your Heart

In the practice of Dharma, there are many methods; if you know their point, they will not lead you astray. However, if you are a practitioner who does not properly respect virtue and a collected mind, you will not succeed, because you are bypassing the Path followed by the great forest masters of the past. Do not disregard these basics. If you wish to practice, you should establish virtue, concentration, and wisdom in your mind and aspire to the Three Gems—Buddha, Dharma, and Sangha. Stop all activity, be an honest person, and go to it. Although various things deceive you time after time, if you are aware of them, you will eventually be able to drop them. The same old person comes telling the same old lies; if you know it, you need not believe him. But it takes a long time before you know; our habits are ever striving to deceive.

When I had been practicing for only two or three years, I still could not trust myself. But after I had experienced much, I learned to trust my own heart. When you have this deep understanding, whatever occurs, you can let it occur, and all things will pass on and be quelled. You will reach a point where the heart tells itself what to do; it is constantly prodding, constantly mindful. Your only concern need be to continue contemplating.

Why Do You Practice?

A group of travelers came to visit Achaan Chah with three elegant questions: Why do you practice? How do you practice? What is the result of your practice? They were sent as a delegation by a European religious organization to ask these questions to a series of great masters throughout Asia.

Achaan Chah closed his eyes, waited, and then answered with three questions of his own: Why do you eat? How do you eat? How do you feel after you have eaten well? Then he laughed.

Later, he explained that we already understand and that teaching has to direct students back to their own inner wisdom, to their own natural Dharma. Therefore, he had reflected the search of these men throughout Asia back to the greater search within.

Let the Tree Grow

The Buddha taught that with things that come about of their own, once you have done your work, you can leave the results to nature, to the power of your accumulated karma. Yet your exertion of effort should not cease. Whether the fruit of wisdom comes quickly or slowly, you cannot force it, just as you cannot force the growth of a tree you have planted. The tree has its own pace. Your job is to dig a hole, water and fertilize it, and protect it from insects. That much is your affair, a matter of faith. But the way the tree grows is up to the tree. If you practice like this, you can be sure all will be well, and your plant will grow.

Thus, you must understand the difference between your work and the plant's work. Leave the plant's business to the plant, and be responsible for your own. If the mind does not know what it needs to do, it will try to force the plant to grow and flower and give fruit in one day. This is wrong view, a major cause of suffering. Just practice in the right direction and leave the rest to your karma. Then, whether it takes one or one hundred or one thousand lifetimes, your practice will be at peace.

Too Much of a Good Thing

When Achaan Chah arrived at a new American meditation center, the many Western students there were quickly charmed and impressed by his teaching. He was clear and direct yet loving and humorous as he poked fun at people's fears and attachments. It was exciting to have such a skillful and famous master visit. The new stories, golden-robed monks, and fresh expressions of Dharma were all wonderful. "Please do not go as soon as you planned, do try to stay a long time," the students requested. "We are so happy to have you."

Achaan Chah smiled. "Of course, things are nice when they are new. But if I stay and teach and make you work, you will get tired of me, won't you? How is your practice when the excitement wears off? You would be bored with me before long. How does this restless, wanting mind stop? Who can teach you that? There only can you learn the real Dharma."

PART III
Our Life Is Our Practice

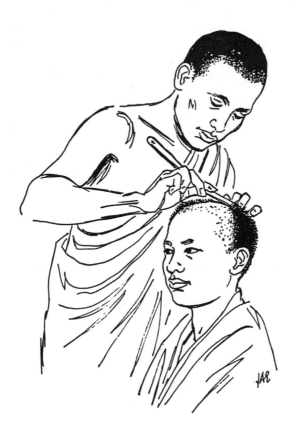

Meditation is not separate from the rest of life. All situations provide opportunity to practice, to grow in wisdom and compassion. Achaan Chah teaches that the right effort for us is to be mindful in all circumstances without running away from the world but to learn to act without grasping or attachment.

Furthermore, he insists that the foundation of a spiritual life is virtue. Although virtue is neglected in our modern society, it must be understood and honored as a fundamental part of meditation. Virtue means taking care so that we do not harm other beings by thought, word, or deed. This respect and caring puts us into a harmonious relationship with all life around us. Only when our words and deeds come from kindness can we quiet the mind and open the heart. The practice of non-harming is the way to begin turning all life situations into practice.

To further establish our lives on the Middle Way, Achaan Chah recommends moderation and self-reliance. A life of excess is difficult soil for the growth of wisdom. To take care with the basics—such as moderation in eating, sleeping, and in speech—helps bring the inner life into balance. It also develops the power of self-reliance. Don't imitate the way others practice or compare yourself to them, Achaan Chah cautions; just let them be. It is hard enough to watch your own mind, so why add the burden of judging others. Learn to use your own breath and everyday life as the place of meditation and you will surely grow in wisdom.

Meditation in Action

Proper effort is not the effort to make something particular happen. It is the effort to be aware and awake in each moment, the effort to overcome laziness and defilement, the effort to make each activity of our day meditation.

To Grasp a Snake

"Our practice here is not to grasp anything," Achaan Chah told a new monk.

"But isn't it necessary to hold onto things sometimes?" the monk protested.

"With the hands, yes, but not with the heart," the teacher replied. "When the heart grasps what is painful, it is like being bitten by a snake. And when, through desire, it grasps what is pleasant, it is just grasping the tail of the snake. It only takes a little while longer for the head of the snake to come around and bite you.

"Make this nongrasping and mindfulness the guardian of your heart, like a parent. Then your likes and dislikes will come calling like children. 'I don't like that, Mommy. I want more of that, Daddy.' Just smile and say, 'Sure, kid.' 'But Mommy, I really want an elephant.' 'Sure, kid.' 'I want candy. Can we go for an airplane ride?' There is no problem if you can let them come and go without grasping."

Something contacts the senses; like or dislike arises; and right there is delusion. Yet with mindfulness, wisdom can arise in this same experience.

Do not fear places where many things contact the senses, if you must be there. Enlightened does not mean being deaf and blind. Saying a mantra every second to block things out, you may get hit by a car. Just be mindful and do not be fooled. When others say something is pretty, say to yourself, "It's not." When others say something is delicious, say to yourself, "No, it's not." Do not get caught in the attachments of the world or in relative judgments. Just let it all go by.

Some people are afraid of generosity. They feel that they will be exploited or oppressed, that they will not be properly caring for themselves. In cultivating generosity, we are only oppressing our greed and attachment. This allows our true nature to express itself and become lighter and freer.

Virtue

There are two levels of practice. The first is the foundation, a development of precepts, virtue, or morality in order to bring happiness, comfort, and harmony among people. The second, more intensive and unconcerned with comfort is the practice of Buddha Dharma directed solely toward awakening, toward the liberation of the heart. This liberation is the source of wisdom and compassion and the true reason for the Buddha's teaching. Understanding these two levels is the basis for true practice.

Virtue and morality are the mother and father of the Dharma growing within us, providing it with the proper nourishment and direction.

Virtue is the basis for a harmonious world in which people can live truly as humans, not animals. Developing virtue is at the heart of our practice. It is very simple. Keep the training precepts. Do not kill, steal, lie, commit sexual misdeeds, or take intoxicants that make you heedless. Cultivate compassion and a reverence for all life. Take care with your goods, your possessions, your actions, your speech. Use virtue to make your life simple and pure. With virtue as a basis for everything you do, your mind will become kind,

clear, and quiet. Meditation will grow easily in this
soil.

The Buddha said, "Refrain from what is bad, do
good, and purify the heart." Our practice, then, is to
get rid of what is worthless and keep what is
valuable. Do you still have anything bad or unskillful
in your heart? Of course! So why not clean house?

As true practice, this getting rid of bad and
cultivating good is fine, but limited. Finally, we must
step over and beyond both good and bad. In the end,
there is a freedom that includes all and a desirelessness
from which love and wisdom naturally flow.

Right effort and virtue are not a question of what
you do outwardly but of constant inner awareness
and restraint. Thus, charity, if given with good intention, can bring happiness to oneself and others. But
virtue must be the root of this charity for it to be
pure.

When those who do not understand the Dharma act
improperly, they look left and right to make sure no
one is looking. How foolish! The Buddha, the Dharma, our karma, are always watching. Do you think
the Buddha cannot see that far? We never really get
away with anything.

Take care of your virtue as a gardener takes care of
trees. Do not be attached to big and small, important
and unimportant. Some people want shortcuts—they
say, "Forget concentration, we'll go straight to insight;
forget virtue, we'll start with concentration." We have
so many excuses for our attachment.

We must start right here where we are, directly and simply. When the first two steps, virtue and right views, have been completed, then the third step, uprooting defilement, will naturally occur without deliberation. When light is produced, we no longer worry about getting rid of darkness, nor do we wonder where the darkness has gone. We just know that there is light.

Following the precepts has three levels. The first is to undertake them as training rules given to us by our teachers. The second arises when we undertake and abide in them by ourselves. But for those at the highest level, the Noble Ones, it is not even necessary to think of precepts, of right or wrong. This true virtue comes from the wisdom that knows the Four Noble Truths in the heart and acts from this understanding.

The Spiral of Virtue, Concentration and Wisdom

The Buddha taught a way out of suffering—the causes of suffering and a practical path. In my practice, I just know this simple path—good in the beginning as virtue, good in the middle as concentration, good in the end as wisdom. If you carefully consider these three, you will see that they actually merge into one.

Let us then consider these three related factors. How does one practice virtue? Actually, in developing virtue, one must begin with wisdom. Traditionally, we speak of keeping precepts, establishing virtue, first. Yet for virtue to be complete, there must be wisdom to understand the full implications of virtue. To start, you must examine your body and speech, investigating the process of cause and effect. If you contemplate body and speech to see in what ways they can cause harm, you will begin to understand, control, and purify both cause and effect.

If you know the characteristics of what is skillful and unskillful in physical and verbal behavior, you already see where to practice in order to give up what is unskillful and do what is good. When you give up wrong and set yourself right, the mind becomes firm, unswerving, concentrated. This concentration limits wavering and doubt as to body and speech. With the mind collected, when forms or sounds come, you can contemplate and see them clearly. By not letting your mind wander, you will see the nature of all experiences according to the truth. When this knowledge is continuous, wisdom arises.

Virtue, concentration, and wisdom, then, can be taken together as one. When they mature, they become synonymous--that is the Noble Path. When greed, hatred, and delusion arise, only this Noble Path is capable of destroying them.

Virtue, concentration, and wisdom can be developed in support of each other, then, like a spiral ever revolving, relying on sights, sounds, smells, tastes, touches, and mind objects. Then whatever arises, Path is always in control. If Path is strong, it destroys the defilements—greed, hatred, and ignorance. If it is weak, mental defilements can gain control, killing this mind of ours. Sights, sounds, and so on arise, and not knowing the truth of them, we allow them to destroy us.

Path and defilement walk side by side in this way. The student of Dharma must always contend with both of them, as if there were two persons fighting. When the Path takes control, it strengthens awareness and contemplation. If you are able to remain aware, defilement will admit defeat when it enters the contest again. If your effort is straight on the Path, it keeps destroying defilement. But if you are weak, when Path is weak, defilement takes over, bringing grasping, illusion, and sorrow. Suffering arises when virtues, concentration, and wisdom are weak.

Once suffering has arisen, that which could have extinguished these sorrows has vanished. Only virtue, concentration, and wisdom can cause Path to arise again. When these are developed, the Path starts functioning continuously, destroying the cause for the arising of suffering in each moment and each situation.

This struggle continues until one side conquers, and the matter can be brought to an end. Thus, I advise practicing unceasingly.

Practice begins here and now. Suffering and liberation, the entire Path, are here and now. The teachings, words like virtue and wisdom, only point to the mind. But these two elements, Path and defilement, compete in the mind all the way to the end of the Path. Therefore, applying the tools of practice is burdensome, difficult—you must rely on endurance, patience, and proper effort. Then true understanding will come about on its own.

Virtue, concentration, and wisdom together constitute the Path. But this Path is not yet the true teaching, not what the teacher actually wanted, but merely the Path that will take one there. For example, say you traveled the road from Bangkok to Wat Ba Pong; the road was necessary for your journey, but you were seeking the monastery, not the road. In the same way, we can say that virtue, concentration, and wisdom are outside the truth of the Buddha but are the road that leads to this truth. When you have developed these three factors, the result is the most wonderful peace. In this peace, sights or sounds have no power to disturb the mind. There is nothing at all left to be done. Therefore, the Buddha says to give up whatever you are holding on to, without anxiety. Then you can know this peace for yourself and will no longer need to believe anyone else. Ultimately, you will come to experience the Dharma of the Noble Ones.

However, do not try to measure your development quickly. Just practice. Otherwise, whenever the mind becomes calm, you will ask, "Is this it?" As soon as you think like this, the whole effort is lost. There are no signs to attest to your progress, like the one that says, "This is the path to Wat Ba Pong." Just throw away all desires and expectations and look directly at the ways of the mind.

What Is Natural?

Claiming they want their practice to be "natural,"
some people complain that this way of life does not fit
their nature.

Nature is the tree in the forest. But if you build a
house, it is no longer natural, is it? Yet if you learn
to use the tree, making wood and building a house, it
has more value to you. Or perhaps the dog is natural,
running here and there, following its nose. Throw
food to dogs and they rush to it, fighting each other.
Is that what you want to be like?

The true meaning of natural can be discovered with
our disciplne and practice. This natural is beyond our
habits, our conditioning, our fears. If the human mind
is left to so-called natural impulses, untrained, it is full
of greed, hatred, and delusion and suffers accordingly.
Yet through practice we can allow our wisdom and
love to grow naturally until it blossoms in any surroundings.

Moderation

Three basic points of practice to work with are sense restraint, which means taking care not to indulge and attach to sensations; moderation in eating; and wakefulness.

Sense restraint. We can easily recognize physical irregularities, such as blindness, deafness, deformed limbs, but irregularities of mind are another matter. When you begin to meditate, you see things differently. You can see the mental distortions that formerly seemed normal, and you can see danger where you did not see it before. This brings sense restraint. You become sensitive, like one who enters a forest or jungle and becomes aware of danger from poisonous creatures, thorns, and so forth. One with a raw wound is likewise more aware of danger from flies and gnats. For one who meditates, the danger is from sense objects. Sense restraint is thus necessary; in fact, it is the highest kind of virtue.

Moderation in eating. It is easy to fast, more difficult to eat little or in moderation as a meditation. Instead of frequent fasting, learn to eat with mindfulness and sensitivity to your needs, learn to distinguish needs from desires.

Pushing the body is not in itself self-torment. Going without sleep or without food may seem extreme at times, but it can have value. We must be willing to resist laziness and defilement, to stir them up and watch them. Once these are understood, such practices are no longer necessary. This is why we should eat, sleep, and talk little—for the purpose of opposing our desires and making them reveal themselves.

Wakefulness. To establish awareness, effort is required constantly, not just when you feel diligent. Even if you meditate all night at times, it is not correct practice if at other times you still follow your laziness. Constantly watch over the mind as a parent watches over a child. Protect it from its own foolishness, teach it what is right.

It is incorrect to think that at certain times you do not have the opportunity to meditate. You must constantly make the effort to know yourself; it is as necessary as your breathing, which continues in all situations. If you do not like certain activities, such as chanting or working, and give up on them as meditation, you will never learn wakefulness.

Rely on Yourself

The Buddha taught that those who wish to know
must realize the truth for themselves. Then it makes
no difference whether others criticize or praise you—
whatever they say, you will be undisturbed. If a person has no trust in himself, when someone calls him
bad, he will feel he is bad accordingly. What a waste
of time! If people call you bad, just examine yourself.
If they are not correct, just ignore them; if they are
correct, learn from them. In either case, why get
angry? If you can see things this way, you will really
be at peace. There will be nothing wrong, there will
be only Dharma. If you really use the tools the Buddha gave us, you need never envy others. Whereas
lazy people want to just listen and believe, you will be
self-sufficient, able to earn your living by your own
efforts.

To practice using only your own resources is
troublesome because they are your own. You once
thought practice was difficult because you were con-
tending, grabbing at others' goods. Then the Buddha
taught you to work with your own, and you thought
everything would be fine. Now you find that too is
difficult, so the Buddha teaches you further. If you
cling and grasp at something, it does not matter
whose it is. If you reach out and grab a fire in your
neighbor's house, the fire will be hot; if you grab a

fire in your own house, that, too, will be hot. So don't grab at anything.

This is how I practice—what is called the direct way. I do not contend with anyone. If you bring scriptures or psychology to argue with me, I will not argue. I will just show you cause and effect, to let you understand the truth of practice. We must all learn to rely on ourselves.

Don't Imitate

We have to be aware of how people tend to imitate their teachers. They become copies, prints, castings. It is like the story of the king's horse trainer. The old trainer died, so the king hired a new trainer. Unfortunately, this man limped when he walked. New and beautiful horses were brought to him, and he trained them exquisitely—to run, to canter, to pull carriages. But each of the new stallions developed a limp. Finally, the king summoned the trainer, and seeing him limp as he entered the court, he understood everything and immediately hired a new trainer.

As teachers, you must be aware of the force of the examples you set. And, even more important, as students, you must not follow the image, the outer form, of your teacher. He is pointing you back to your own inner perfection. Take the inner wisdom as your model, and do not imitate his limp.

Know Yourself—Know Others

Know your own mind and body, and you will know others' as well. One's facial expressions, speech, gestures, actions, all stem from one's state of mind. A Buddha, an enlightened being, can read these because he has experienced and seen with wisdom the states of mind that underlie them, just as wise older people, having passed through childhood, can understand the ways of children.

This self-knowledge differs from memory. An old person can be clear inside but fuzzy in regard to external things. Book learning may be very difficult for him, he forgets names and faces, and so on. Maybe he knows very well that he wants a basin, but because of the weakness of his memory, he may ask for a glass instead.

If you see states rising and falling in the mind and do not cling to the process, letting go of both happiness and suffering, mental rebirths become shorter and shorter. Letting go, you can even fall into hell states without too much disturbance, because you know the impermanence of them. Through right practice, you allow your old karma to wear itself out. Knowing how things arise and pass away, you can just be aware and let them run their course. It is like having two trees: if you fertilize and water one and do not take care of the other, there is no question which one will grow and which one will die.

Let Others Be

Do not find fault with others. If they behave wrongly, there is no need to make yourself suffer. If you point out to them what is correct and they do not practice accordingly, leave it at that.

When the Buddha studied with various teachers, he realized that their ways were lacking, but he did not disparage them. Studying with humility and respect, he benefited from his relationship with them, yet he realized that their systems were not complete. Still, as he had not yet become enlightened, he did not criticize or attempt to teach them. After he found enlightenment, he respectfully remembered those he had studied with and wanted to share his newfound knowledge with them.

Real Love

Real love is wisdom. What most people think of as love is just an impermanent feeling. If you have a nice taste every day, you will soon get tired of it. In the same way, such love eventually turns into hatred and sorrow. Such worldly happiness involves clinging and is always tied up with suffering, which comes like the policeman following the thief.

Nevertheless, we cannot suppress nor forbid such feelings. We just should not cling to or identify with them but should know them for what they are. Then Dharma is present. One loves another, yet eventually the beloved leaves or dies. To lament and think longingly, grasping after that which has changed, is suffering, not love. When we are at one with this truth and no longer need or desire, wisdom and the real love that transcends desire fill our world.

Learning Through Life

Boredom is not a real problem; if we look closely we can see that the mind is always active. Thus, we always have work to do.

Relying on yourself to do little things—like cleaning up carefully after the meal, doing chores gracefully and mindfully, not banging on kettles—helps develop concentration and makes practice easier. It can also indicate to you whether or not you have really established mindfulness or are still getting lost in defilement.

You Westerners are generally in a hurry; therefore, you will have greater extremes of happiness, suffering, and defilement. If you practice correctly, the fact that you have to deal with many problems can be a source of deep wisdom later on.

Oppose Your Mind

Consider the Buddha's compassion and skill. He taught us after his own enlightenment. Finished with his own business, he got involved in ours, teaching us all these wonderful means. Concerning practice I have followed him, I have made all efforts in seeking, giving up my life to it because I believe in what the Buddha taught—that Path, fruition, and Nirvana exist. But these things are not accidental. They arise from right practice, from right effort, from being bold, daring to train, to think, to adapt, to do. This effort involves opposing your own mind.

The Buddha says not to trust the mind because it is defiled, impure, does not yet embody virtue or Dharma. In all the different practices we do, we must therefore oppose this mind. When the mind is opposed, it becomes hot and distressed, and we begin to wonder whether we are on the right path. Because practice interferes with defilement, with desire, we suffer and may even decide to stop practicing. The Buddha, however, taught that this is the correct practice and that defilement, not you, is the one that is inflamed. Naturally, such practice is difficult.

Some meditation monks only seek the Dharma according to words and books. Of course, when it is time for study, study according to the text. But when you are "fighting" with defilement, fight outside the text. If you fight according to a model, you will not be able to stand up to the enemy. The texts only provide an example and can cause you to lose yourself because they are based on memories and concepts. Conceptual thinking creates illusion and embellishment and can take you to the heavens and hells, to the far reaches of imagination, beyond the simple truth here in front of you.

If you undertake the training, you will find that at first, physical solitude is important. When you come to live in seclusion, you can think of Sariputta's advice to monks concerning physical seclusion, mental seclusion, and seclusion from defilement and temptation. He taught that physical seclusion is the cause for the arising of mental seclusion, and mental seclusion is the cause for the arising of seclusion from defilement. Of course, if your heart is calm, you can live anywhere, but in first beginning to know Dharma, physical seclusion is invaluable. Today, or any day, go and sit far away from the village. Try it, staying alone. Or go to some fearful hilltop by yourself. Then you can begin to know what it is really like to look at yourself.

Whether or not there is tranquillity, do not be concerned. As long as you are practicing, you are creating right causes and will be able to make use of whatever arises. Do not be afraid that you will not succeed, will not become tranquil. If you practice sincerely, you must grow in Dharma. Those who seek will see, just as those who eat will be satisfied.

Just Let Go

Do everything with a mind that lets go. Do not expect any praise or reward. If you let go a little, you will have a little peace. If you let go a lot, you will have a lot of peace. If you let go completely, you will know complete peace and freedom. Your struggles with the world will have come to an end.

PART IV
Meditation and Formal Practice

In keeping with his general style of teaching, the
meditation instructions of Achaan Chah are simple
and natural. Usually he just tells people to sit and
watch their breath or to walk and notice their body.
Then, after a while, he asks them to begin to examine
their heart and mind in both postures, to see their
nature and characteristics. Sometimes this is all that is
offered for initial instruction.

Achaan Chah is careful to avoid letting any method
of practice be confused with Dharma. The Dharma is
what is, and Dharma practice is any way that clearly
apprehends the true nature and characteristics of what
is, of our world, of body and mind. Therefore,
Achaan Chah does not emphasize any particular
technique. He wants students to learn inner strength
and independence in practice from the beginning, asking questions when necessary, but relying on their
own ability to watch and understand the mind and on
their own wisdom to illuminate their experience.

Still, after being at Wat Ba Pong for some time,
practicing alone, learning from some of the senior
monks, and hearing many questions answered and
many Dharma talks, one learns certain subtleties of
formal practice. A variety of traditional forest meditations such as the simple mantra "Buddho," or
cemetary meditations, or contemplations on the
thirty-two parts of the body are also taught when
deemed appropriate for particular students. Otherwise, meditation is developed in a simple and
straightforward fashion.

In sitting practice, Achaan Chah says it is best to sit
with a balanced and erect posture, legs crossed or in
some other position that keeps the back and head
straight and the chest open for unrestricted breathing.
One should sit quite still, allowing the body to

become settled and quiet in preparation for the initial breathing meditation.

The first direction of sitting practice is to still and concentrate the mind. Focus the attention on the breath in an easy and natural way, allowing it to come and go without interference. Use the sensation, the direct experience of the breath as it enters and leaves the nostrils, as the point of concentration. Silently follow the sensation of the breath for as long as you can. Then, each time you notice the mind has wandered (which will be thousands of times until it is trained), return gently to concentration on the breath.

This meditation is a way of using our most immediate experience, the ever-changing reality of the breath, to concentrate the mind. One is instructed to patiently continue this simple exercise as a way of strengthening the power of the mind to focus and see. Eventually, this very simple breath concentration can lead to the highest levels of meditative absorption and samadhi.

However, absorption is not the goal of the practice as taught by Achaan Chah, even though for some it may arise naturally in the course of meditation. Students are instructed to use the concentration and stillness they develop through mindfulness of breathing to aid in the second aspect of their practice. Once the mind is somewhat quiet and focused, one is instructed to begin to examine the workings of the mind and body. To examine or to contemplate does not mean to think about, but rather to feel, to experience directly, how our world is happening. Examine the aggregates of body and mind, Achaan Chah often advises. Notice first the body, which is directly experienced as an ever-changing play of senses, of elements—hot, cold, bright, dark, soft, hard, heavy,

light, and so on. Examine the aggregates of feeling—
pleasant, neutral, and unpleasant—changing each moment. Notice the play of perception, of memory and
thought, of reactions and volition, of consciousness,
the quality each of these experiences brings anew in
each moment. See how life is a dynamic interplay of
these aggregates arising, changing, passing away.
Sense objects, feeling, recognition, reaction, volition,
the same process again and again. Notice what experience is like when desire or expectation arises.
Notice the causes of suffering. Notice the stillness
when the mind is not caught by desire.

Is there any part of experience that does not share
the characteristics of constant change and fleeting in-
stability, any part that gives lasting satisfaction and is
not empty of a self, of an I, of an ego? Where is the
self in all this? Examine and you will see how ab-
solutely everything is changing. No me exists, no fixed
self. Only this process.

To learn to see deeply into experience and its
characteristics is not limited to sitting meditation.
Walk and watch. Do the walking meditation back and
forth at a natural pace; do it for many hours, if possible. Learn to pay attention, and there is nothing you
will not understand. This is the heart of the practice.

In many monasteries, daily interviews with the
teacher are an integral part of the practice, but
Achaan Chah discourages this. Although he is always
available to answer questions, he does not conduct
formal interviews. Learning to answer your own question is better, he says. Learn about doubting in the
mind, how it arises and how it passes. No one and
nothing can free you but your own understanding.
Still the mind, the heart, and learn to watch. You will
find the whole Dharma of the Buddha is revealing
itself in every moment.

Mindfulness

Just as animal life can be classified into two groups, creatures of the land and creatures of the sea, subjects of meditation can be divided into two categories, concentration and insight. Concentration meditations are those that are used to make the mind calm and one-pointed. Insight, on the one hand, is the growing perception of impermanence, suffering, and emptiness of self and, on the other, our bridge over those waters.

No matter how we may feel about our existence, our business is not to try to change it in any way. Rather, we just have to see it and let it be. Where suffering is, there too is the way out of suffering. Seeing that which is born and dies and is subject to suffering, Buddha knew there must also be something beyond birth and death, free of suffering.

Methods of meditation all have value in helping to develop mindfulness. The point is to use mindfulness to see the underlying truth. With this mindfulness, we watch all desires, likes and dislikes, pleasures and pains that arise in the mind. Realizing they are impermanent, suffering, and empty of self, we let go of them. In this way, wisdom replaces ignorance, knowledge replaces doubt.

As for singling out one object of meditation, you yourself must discover what fits your character. Wherever you choose to be mindful, it will bring wisdom to the mind. Mindfulness is knowing what is here, noticing, being aware. Clear comprehension knows the context in which the present is occurring. When mindfulness and clear comprehension act together, their companion, wisdom, always appears to help them complete any task.

Watch the mind, watch the process of experience arising and ceasing. At first the movement is constant —as soon as one thing passes, another arises, and we seem to see more arising than ceasing. As time goes by we see more clearly, understanding how things arise so fast, until we reach the point where they arise, cease, and do not arise again.

With mindfulness you can see the real owner of things. Do you think this is your world, your body? It is the world's world, the body's body. If you tell it, Don't get old, does the body listen? Does your stomach ask permission to get sick? We only rent this house; why not find out who really owns it?

The Essence of Vipassana: Observing Your Mind

Begin practice by sitting up straight and paying attention. You can sit on the floor, you can sit in a chair. At first, you need not fix your attention on much. Simply be mindful of in-and-out breathing. If you find it helpful, you can also repeat "Buddho," "Dharmo," or "Sangho" as a mantra while you watch the breath going in and out. In this awareness of breathing, you must not force. If you try to control your breathing, that is not yet correct. It may seem that the breathing is too short, too long, too gentle, too heavy. You may feel that you are not passing the breath properly, or you may not feel well. Just let it be, let it settle by itself. Eventually the breath will enter and exit freely. When you are aware of and firmly established in this entry and exit, that is correct breathing.

When you become distracted, stop and refocus your attention. At first, when you are focusing it, your mind wants it to be a certain way. But do not control it or worry about it. Just notice it and let it be. Keep at it. Samadhi will grow by itself. As you go on practicing in this way, sometimes the breath will stop, but here again, do not fear. Only your perception of the breath has stopped; the subtle factors continue. When the time is right, the breath will come back on its own as before.

If you can make your mind tranquil like this, wherever you find yourself—on a chair, in a car, on a boat—you will be able to fix your attention and enter into a calm state immediately. Wherever you are, you will be able to sit for meditation.

Having reached this point, you know something of the Path, but you must also contemplate sense objects. Turn your tranquil mind toward sights, sounds, smells, tastes, touches, thoughts, mental objects, mental factors. Whatever arises, investigate it. Notice whether you like it or not, whether it pleases or displeases you, but do not get involved with it. This liking and disliking are just reactions to the world of appearances—you must see a deeper level. Then, whether something initially seems good or bad, you will see that it is really only impermanent, unsatisfactory, and empty. File everything that arises into those three categories—good, bad, evil, wonderful, whatever it is, put it there. This is the way of vipassana, by which all things are calmed.

Before long, knowledge and insight into impermanence, unsatisfactoriness, and emptiness will arise. This is the beginning of true wisdom, the heart of meditation, which leads to liberation. Follow your experience. See it. Strive continuously. Know the truth. Learn to give up, to get rid, to attain peace.

When sitting in meditation, you may have strange experiences or visions such as seeing lights, angels, or buddhas. When you see such things, you should observe yourself first to find out what state the mind is in. Do not forget the basic point. Pay attention. Do not wish for visions to arise or not to arise. If you go running after such experiences, you may end up babbling senselessly because the mind has fled the stable.

When such things do come, contemplate them. When you have contemplated them, do not be deluded by them. You should consider that they are not yourself; they too are impermanent, unsatisfactory, and not self. Though they have come about, do not take them seriously. If they do not go away, re-establish your mindfulness, fix your attention on your breathing, and take at least three long inhalations and exhalations—then you can cut them off. Whatever arises, keep re-establishing your attention. Do not take anything as yourself—everything is only a vision or a construction of the mind, a deception that causes you to like, grasp, or fear. When you see such constructions, do not get involved. All unusual experiences and visions are of value to the wise person but harmful to the unwise. Keep practicing until you are not stirred by them.

If you can trust your mind in this way, there is no problem. If it wants to be glad, you just know that this gladness is uncertain, unstable. Do not fear your visions or other experiences in practice, just learn to work with them. In this way, defilement can be used to train the mind, and you come to know the natural state of the mind, free from extremes, clear, unattached.

As I see it, the mind is like a single point, the center of the universe, and mental states are like visitors who come to stay at this point for short or long periods of time. Get to know these visitors well. Become familiar with the vivid pictures they paint, the alluring stories they tell, to entice you to follow them. But do not give up your seat—it is the only chair around. If you continue to occupy it unceasingly, greeting each guest as it comes, firmly establishing yourself in awareness, transforming your mind into the one who knows, the one who is awake, the visitors will eventually stop coming back. If you give them real attention, how many times can these visitors return? Speak with them here, and you will know every one of them well. Then your mind will at last be at peace.

Walking Meditation

Work with the walking meditation every day. To begin, clasp the hands in front of you, maintaining a very slight tension that compels the mind to be attentive. Walk at a normal pace from one end of the path to the other, knowing yourself all the way. Stop and return. If the mind wanders, stand still and bring it back. If the mind still wanders, fix attention on the breath. Keep coming back. Mindfulness thus developed is useful at all times.

Change positions when physically tired, but not as soon as you feel an impulse to change. First, know why you want to change—is it physical fatigue, mental restlessness, or laziness? Notice the sufferings of the body. Learn to watch openly and carefully. Effort in practice is a matter of the mind, not the body. It means constantly being aware of what goes on in the mind without following like and dislike as they arise. Sitting or walking all night is not in itself energetic effort if one is not aware in this way.

As you walk from one predetermined point to another, fix the eyes about two yards in front of you and fix the attention on the actual feeling of the body, or repeat the mantra "Buddho." Do not fear things that arise in the mind; question them, know them. The truth is more than thoughts and feelings, so do not believe and get caught by them. See the whole process arising and ceasing. This understanding gives rise to wisdom.

When consciousness arises, we should have awareness of it at the same time, like a light bulb and its light. If you are not alert, the hindrances will catch hold of the mind—only concentration can cut through them. Just as the presence of a thief prevents negligence with our possessions, so the reminder of the hindrances should prevent negligence in our concentration.

Who Is Sick?

Late in the spring of 1979, Achaan Chah visited the Insight Meditation Center in Barre, Massachusetts. He taught there for ten days and each afternoon would go for a walk around the grounds. Seeing all the students out on the lawns doing slow walking meditation, he remarked that the meditation center looked like a mental hospital for the diseases of the worldly mind. All afternoon as he wandered past students, he would call out to them, "Get well soon. I hope you get well soon."

Because people react differently, we must pick suitable practices. Body practices are especially suitable for persons with excessive lust or for forest monks.

In the body meditations, look at the body. See its parts, its real constituents. Start with the head, hair, body hair, nails, teeth, skin, see it everywhere. Separate them from the other body parts. Mentally peel off the skin, and see the inside. Do you want it? Seeing the true nature of the body can cut off the first three fetters:

1. Own-body view, sense of self. We will see that it is neither us nor ours, that nothing in this world is ours.
2. Skeptical doubt. Knowing things as they are puts an end to doubt.

3. Attachment to a path based on rites and ritual. While still in doubt, we may think, "Perhaps this way is not so good." But once we see clearly what the body is—that it, like all things, is impermanent, unsatisfactory, and empty of self—this uncertainty is cleared up.

When meditating on the body, you need not contemplate all its thirty-two parts. If you concentrate on one and see it as it is—impermanent, unsatisfactory, empty, unclean—you will see that your body and the bodies of others are like this. If there are thirty-two ice cubes, you need only touch one to know the coldness of all.

When we develop the meditation on the impurity of the body, we are also developing the meditation on death. Indeed, when we develop one of the Dharmas, we develop them all. If we understand the fact of our own death, we can become very sensitive to all life in the world. We will naturally avoid wrongdoing and want to spend our days wisely, feeling a common bond with all beings.

Learning Concentration

In our practice, we think that noises, cars, voices, sights, are distractions that come and bother us when we want to be quiet. But who is bothering whom? Actually, we are the ones who go and bother them. The car, the sound, is just following its own nature. We bother things through some false idea that they are outside us and cling to the ideal of remaining quiet, undisturbed.

Learn to see that it is not things that bother us, that we go out to bother them. See the world as a mirror. It is all a reflection of mind. When you know this, you can grow in every moment, and every experience reveals truth and brings understanding.

Normally, the untrained mind is full of worries and anxieties, so when a bit of tranquillity arises from practicing meditation, you easily become attached to it, mistaking states of tranquillity for the end of meditation. Sometimes you may even think you have put an end to lust or greed or hatred, only to be overwhelmed by them later on. Actually, it is worse to be caught in calmness than to be stuck in agitation, because at least you will want to escape from agitation, whereas you are content to remain in calmness and not go any further.

When extraordinarily blissful, clear states arise from insight meditation practice, do not cling to them.

Although this tranquillity has a sweet taste, it too must be seen as impermanent, unsatisfactory, and empty. Absorption is not what the Buddha found essential in meditation. Practice without thought of attaining absorption or any special state. Just know whether the mind is calm or not and, if so, whether a little or a lot. In this way it will develop on its own.

Nevertheless, concentration must be firmly established for wisdom to arise. To concentrate the mind is like turning on the switch, and wisdom is the resulting light. Without the switch, there is no light, but we should not waste our time playing with the switch. Likewise, concentration is the empty bowl and wisdom the food that fills it and makes the meal.

Do not be attached to the object of meditation such as a mantra. Know its purpose. If you succeed in concentrating your mind using the mantra "Buddho," let the mantra go. It is a mistake to think that to stop repeating "Buddho" would be laziness. *Buddho* means "the one who knows"—if you become one who knows, why repeat the word?

Stick To It

Endurance and moderation are the foundation, the beginning of our practice. To start we simply follow the practice and the schedule set up by ourself or in a retreat or monastery. To train an animal, we have to restrain it; likewise, we need to restrict ourselves. An animal which is difficult to train should be given little food. Here we have the ascetic practices to limit ourselves in regard to food, robes, and living quarters, to bring us down to bare essentials, to cut away infatuation.

These practices are the basis for concentration. Constant mindfulness in all postures and activities will make the mind calm and clear. But this calm is not the end point of practice. Tranquil states give the mind a temporary rest, as eating will temporarily remove hunger, but that is not all there is to life. You must use the calmed mind to see things in a new light, the light of wisdom. When the heart becomes firm in this wisdom, you will not adhere to worldly standards of good and bad and will not be swayed by external conditions. With wisdom, dung can be used for fertilizer—all our experiences become sources of insight. Normally, we want praise and dislike criticism, but, seen with a clear mind, we see them as equally empty. Thus, we can let go of all these things and find peace.

Do not worry about how long it will take to get results, just do it. Practice endurance. If your legs hurt, tell yourself, "I have no legs." If your head aches, think, "I do not have a head." If you get sleepy when sitting at night, think, "It is daytime." During meditation using mindfulness of breathing, if you have uncomfortable feelings in the chest, take a few long, deep breaths. If the mind wanders, just hold your breath and let the mind go where it will—it will not go far.

You can change postures after an appropriate time, but do not be a slave to your restlessness or feelings of discomfort. Sometimes it is good just to sit on them. You feel hot, legs are painful, you are unable to concentrate—just tell it all to die. The feelings will get more and more intense and then hit a breaking point, after which you will be calm and cool. But the next day your mind will not want to do it again. Training yourself requires constant effort. By practicing over a long period of time, you will learn when to push, when to relax, learn to separate physical fatigue from laziness.

Do not worry about enlightenment. When growing a tree, you plant it, water it, fertilize it, keep the bugs away and if these things are done properly, the tree will naturally grow. How quickly it grows, however, is something you cannot control.

At first, endurance and persistence are necessary, but after a time, faith and certainty arise. Then you see the value of practice and want to do it; you want to avoid socializing and be by yourself in quiet places; you seek extra time just to practice and to study yourself.

Just do the practice beginning with the basic steps —being honest and clean and being aware of whatever you do. All the rest will follow.

Seven Days to Enlightenment

Achaan Chah described how the Buddha had encouraged his monks by stating that those who practiced diligently would surely be enlightened in seven days or, if not in seven days, then in seven months or seven years. A young American monk heard this and asked if it was still true. Achaan Chah promised that if the young monk was continuously mindful without break for only seven days, he would be enlightened.

Excitedly the young monk started his seven days, only to be lost in forgetfulness ten minutes later. Coming back to himself, he again started his seven days, only to become lost once more in mindless thought—perhaps about what he would do after his enlightenment. Again and again he began his seven days, and again and again he lost his continuity of mindfulness. A week later, he was not enlightened but had become very much aware of his habitual fantasies and wandering of mind—a most instructive way to begin his practice on the Path to real awakening.

Results should not be expected too quickly. One with faith and confidence will have determination to persevere, as a market woman who wants to sell goods keeps on hawking, "Who wants soap? Who wants baskets? I've got pencils to sell."

Learning to Chant

A principal part of Achaan Chah's training is to help students learn to do whatever task is appropriate while keeping a balanced mind free from clinging. A Western psychiatrist who had ordained as a monk had to learn this lesson. He asked permission to stay at Wat Ba Pong for the three-month rains retreat in order to have a master under whom he could really practice meditation. Several days later, when Achaan Chah announced to the assembled monks that chanting of the sutras from 3:30 to 4:40 A.M. and from 5:00 to 6:00 P.M. was a mandatory part of the rains retreat, this newly ordained Western monk raised his hand and began to argue loudly that he had come to meditate, not to waste time chanting. Such a Western-style argument with the teacher in public was a shock to many of the other monks. Achaan Chah explained calmly that real meditation had to do with attitude and awareness in any activity, not just with seeking silence in a forest cottage. He made a point of insisting that the psychiatrist would have to be prompt for every chanting session for the entire rains retreat if he wished to stay at Wat Ba Pong. The psychiatrist stayed and learned to chant beautifully.

Forget About Time

We tend to complicate our meditation. For example, when we sit, we may determine, "Yes, I'm really going to do it this time." But that is not the right attitude; nothing will be accomplished that day. Such grasping is natural at first. Some nights, when I would start to sit, I would think, "OK, tonight I won't get up from my seat until 1:00 A.M., at the earliest." But before long, my mind would start to kick and rebel until I felt that I would die. What is the point in that?

When you are sitting properly, there is no need to measure or compel. There is no goal, no point to attain. Whether you sit until 7:00 or 8:00 or 9:00 P.M., never mind. Just keep sitting without concern. Do not force yourself. Do not be compulsive. Do not command your heart to do things for certain, for this command will make things all the less certain. Let your mind be at ease, let your breath be even, normal, not short or long or any special way. Let your body be comfortable. Practice steadily and continuously. Desire will ask you, "How late will we go? How long will we practice?" Just shout at it, "Hey, don't bother me!" Keep quelling it, because it is only defilement coming to disturb you. Just say, "If I want to stop early or late, it's not wrong; if I want to sit all night, who am I hurting? Why do you come and disturb me?" Cut off desire, and keep sitting in your own way. Let your heart be at ease, and you will become tranquil, free from the power of grasping.

Some people sit in front of a lighted incense stick and vow to sit until it has burned down. Then they keep peeking to see how far it has burned, constantly concerned with the time. "Is it over yet?" they ask. Or they vow to push beyond or die, and then feel terribly guilty when they stop only one hour later. These people are controlled by desire.

Do not pay attention to the time. Just maintain your practice at a steady pace, letting it progress gradually. You do not need to make vows. Just keep striving to train yourself, just do your practice and let the mind become calm of itself. Eventually, you will find that you can sit a long time at your ease, practicing correctly.

As to pain in the legs, you will find that it goes away by itself. Just stay with your contemplation.

If you practice in this way, a change will take place in you. When you go to sleep, you will be able to settle your mind into calmness and sleep. Formerly, you may have snored, talked in your sleep, gnashed your teeth, or tossed and turned. Once your heart has been trained, all of that will vanish. Although you will sleep soundly, you will awaken refreshed instead of sleepy. The body will rest, but the mind will be awake day and night. This is Buddho, the one who knows, the Awakened One, the Happy One, the Brilliant One. This one does not sleep, does not feel drowsy. If you make your heart and mind firm like this in your practice, you may not sleep for two or three days, and when you get sleepy, you can enter samadhi for five or ten minutes and arise refreshed, as if you had slept all night long. At this point, you need not think about your body, although with compassion and understanding, you will still consider its needs.

Some Hints on Practicing

As you practice, various images and visions may
arise. You see an attractive form, hear a sound that
stirs you—such an image must be observed too. This
kind of vipassana image can have even more energy
than one that may arise from simple concentration.
Whatever arises, just watch.

Someone recently asked me, "As we meditate and
various thing arise in my mind, should we investigate
them or just note them coming and going?" If you see
someone passing by whom you do not know, you
may wonder, "Who is that? Where is he going? What
is he up to?" But if you know the person, it is enough
just to notice him pass by.

Desire in practice can be friend or foe. At first, it
spurs us to come and practice; we want to change
things, to understand, to end suffering. But to be
always desiring something that has not yet arisen, to
want things to be other than they are, just causes
more suffering.

Someone asked, "Should we just eat when hungry,
sleep when tired, as the Zen masters suggest, or
should we experiment by going against the grain at
times? And if so, how much?" Of course, one should
experiment, but no one else can say how much. All of

this is to be known within oneself. At first, in our practice, we are like children learning to write the alphabet. The letters come out bent and sloppy, time and again—the only thing to do is to keep at it. And if we do not live life like this, what else is there for us to do?

A good practice is to ask yourself very sincerely, "Why was I born?" Ask yourself this question three times a day, in the morning, in the afternoon, and at night. Ask everyday.

The Buddha told his disciple Ananda to see impermanence, to see death with every breath. We must know death; we must die in order to live. What does this mean? To die is to come to the end of all our doubts, all our questions, and just be here with the present reality. You can never die tomorrow, you must die now. Can you do it? Ah, how still, the peace of no more questions.

Real effort is a matter of the mind, not of the body. Different methods of concentration are like ways of earning a living—the most important thing is that you feed yourself, not how you manage to get the food. Actually, when the mind is freed from desires, concentration arises naturally, no matter what activity you are engaged in.

Drugs can bring about meaningful experiences, but the one who takes a drug has not made causes for such effects. He has just temporarily altered nature, like injecting a monkey with hormones that send him shooting up a tree to pick coconuts. Such experiences

may be true but not good or good but not true,
whereas Dharma is always both good and true.

Sometimes we want to force the mind to be quiet,
and this effort just makes it all the more disturbed.
Then we stop pushing and some concentration arises.
But in the state of calm and quiet, we begin to wonder, "What's going on? What's happening now?" and
we are agitated again.

The day before the first monastic council, one of
the Buddha's disciples went to tell Ananda, "Tomorrow is the Sangha Council. Others who attend are fully enlightened." Since Ananda was at this time still in-
completely enlightened, he determined to practice
strenuously all through the night, seeking full awakening. But in the end, he just made himself tired. He
was not making any progress for all his efforts, so he
decided to let go and rest a bit. As soon as his head
hit the pillow, he became enlightened. In the end, we
must learn to let go every last desire, even the desire
for enlightenment. Only then can we be free.

Contemplate Everything

As you proceed with your practice, you must be willing to carefully examine every experience, every sense door. For example, practice with a sense object such as a sound. Listen. Your hearing is one thing, the sound is another. You are aware, and that is all there is to it. There is no one, nothing else. Learn to pay careful attention. Rely on nature in this way, and contemplate to find the truth. You will see how things separate themselves. When the mind does not grasp or take a vested interest, does not get caught up, things become clear.

When the ear hears, observe the mind. Does it get caught up and make a story out of the sound? Is it disturbed? You can know this, stay with it, be aware. At times you may want to escape from the sound, but that is not the way out. You must escape through awareness.

Sometimes we like the Dharma, sometimes we do not, but the problem is never the Dharma's. We cannot expect to have tranquillity as soon as we start to practice. We should let the mind think, let it do as it will, just watch it and not react to it. Then, as things contact the senses, we should practice equanimity. See all sense impressions as the same. See how they come and go. Keep the mind in the present. Do not think about what has passed, do not think, "Tomorrow I'm going to do it." If we see the true characteristics of things in the present moment, at all times, then *everything* is Dharma revealing itself.

Train the heart until it is firm, until it lays down all experiences. Then things will come and you will perceive them without becoming attached. You do not have to force the mind and sense objects apart. As you practice, they separate by themselves, showing the simple elements of body and mind.

As you learn about sights, sounds, smells, and tastes according to the truth, you will see that they all have a common nature—impermanent, unsatisfactory, and empty of self. Whenever you hear a sound, it registers in your mind as this common nature. Having heard is the same as not having heard. Mindfulness is constantly with you, protecting the heart. If your heart can reach this state wherever you go, there will be a growing understanding within you. which is called investigation, one of the seven factors of enlightenment. It revolves, it spins, it converses with itself, it solves, it detaches from feelings, perceptions, thoughts, consciousness. Nothing can come near it. It has its own work to do. This awareness is an automatic aspect of the mind that already exists and that you discover when you train in the beginning stages of practice.

Whatever you see, whatever you do, notice everything. Do not put the meditation aside for a rest. Some people think they can stop as soon as they come out of a period of formal practice. Having stopped formal practice, they stop being attentive, stop contemplating. Do not do it that way. Whatever you see, you should contemplate. If you see good people or bad people, rich people or poor people, watch. When you see old people or small children, youngsters or adults, contemplate all of it. This is the heart of our practice.

In contemplating to seek the Dharma, you should observe the characteristics, the cause and effect, the play of all the objects of your senses, big and small, white and black, good and evil. If there is thinking, simply contemplate it as thinking. All these things are impermanent, unsatisfactory, and empty of self, so do not cling to them. Awareness is their graveyard; dump them all here. Then seeing the impermanence and emptiness of all things, you can put an end to suffering. Keep contemplating and examining this life.

Notice what happens when something good comes to you. Are you glad? You should contemplate that gladness. Perhaps you use something for a while and then start to dislike it, wanting to give it or sell it to someone else. If no one comes to buy it, you may even try to throw it away. Why are we like this? Our life is impermanent, constantly subject to change. You must look at its true characteristics. Once you completely understand just one of these incidents, you will understand them all. They are all of the same nature.

Perhaps you do not like a particular sight or sound. Make note of that—later, you may like it, you may become pleased with what formerly displeased you. Such things do happen. When you realize clearly that all such things are impermanent, unsatisfactory, and not self, you will dump them all and attachment will not arise. When you see that all the various things that come to you are the same, there will be only Dharma arising.

Once having entered this stream and tasted liberation, you will not return, you will have gone beyond wrongdoing and wrong understanding. The mind, the heart, will have turned, will have entered the stream, and it will not be able to fall back into suffering again. How could it fall? It has given up unskillful actions because it sees the danger in them and cannot again be made to do wrong in body or speech. It has entered the Way fully, knows its duties, knows its work, knows the Path, knows its own nature. It lets go of what needs to be let go of and keeps letting go without doubting.

All that I have said up to now has merely been words. When people come to see me, I have to say something. But it is best not to speak about these matters too much. Better to begin practice without delay. I am like a good friend inviting you to go somewhere. Do not hesitate, just get going. You won't regret it.

The Leaves Will Always Fall

Every day or two, the open grounds and walkways of the monastery must be swept clear of the leaves that fall in every Asian season. For the large open areas, the monks will team up and, with long-handled bamboo brooms extended, sweep like a dust storm, clearing all the leaves in their path. Sweeping is so satisfying.

All the while, the forest continues to give its teachings. The leaves fall, the monks sweep, and yet, even while the sweeping continues and the near end of a long path is being cleared, the monks can look back to the far end they have already swept and see a new scattering of leaves already starting to cover their work.

"Our lives are like the breath, like the growing and falling leaves," says Achaan Chah. "When we can really understand about falling leaves, we can sweep the paths every day and have great happiness in our lives on this changing earth."

PART V
Lessons in the Forest

Daily life at Wat Ba Pong, as at most forest monasteries, begins at 3:00 A.M. with group chanting and meditation until just before dawn. At dawn monks walk barefoot two to eight miles to collect alms food at various nearby villages. On their return, the food collected is shared equally in begging bowls, and eating of the one daily meal begins with a chanted blessing. After meal clean-up, from 9:30 A.M. to 3:00 P.M. monks return to their huts for a period of solitary meditation, study, or work, or they join various monastery projects, such as repairing buildings and fences, sewing robes, or constructing new cottages. At 3:00 P.M., all are called to help draw and carry well water to the water storage barrels and to sweep the central grounds. At 6:00 P.M., after bathing, the monks reassemble for meditation, evening chanting, and periodic Dharma talks. Returning to their cottages, they use the late evening hours for silent sitting and walking meditation and as a time to listen to the sounds of the forest as it settles down for the night.

The spirit of practice at Wat Ba Pong is to establish right understanding and then apply it with mindfulness to every task and situation. This way of practice is one that can be equally well applied in the midst of any busy life, so the Lessons in the Forest are important ones for us as Westerners too. At the monastery both alms-food collecting and floor cleaning are meditation, and awareness is trained equally in following the breath and in shaving the head. On some days Achaan Chah participates intimately in the daily life of the monastery, cleaning and sweeping leaves with the other monks. On others he teaches more formally, receiving the constant stream of visitors seeking his wisdom and advice.

In all these situations he teaches the monks. Sometimes it is through his presence, his simple, straightforward participation in the round of monastery life. Often it is through his words—humorous comments, practical Dharma points, or answers to questions that arise in the course of a day.

Periodically, Achaan Chah gives an extended evening talk to the assembled monks and lay people on some aspect of practice and spiritual life. The talk may be given in response to a question, for a special visitor, or as a spontaneous teaching. In each case, he sits silently for a moment, closes his eyes, and a natural outflow of Dharma begins.

In many ways he inspires those who share daily life with him in the forest. He shows us that only in walking this path ourselves can we move from theory to realization, from ideas of Dharma to a life of wisdom and compassion.

A Monk's Life

Here in the forest where a monk can learn to contemplate the nature of things, he can live happily and peacefully. As he looks around, he understands that all forms of life degenerate and eventually die. Nothing that exists is permanent, and when he understands this, he begins to become serene.

Monks are trained to be content with little—to eat only what they need, to sleep only when necessary, to be satisfied with what they have. This is the foundation of Buddhist meditation. Buddhist monks do not practice meditation for selfish reasons but in order to know and understand themselves, and thus be able to teach others how to live peacefullly and wisely.

Meditation does not simply involve being at peace with the world. On the contrary, confronting the self can be like walking into a raging storm. Beginning intensive practice, one often despairs at first and may even want to kill oneself. Some think that a monk's life is lazy and easy—let them try it themselves and see how long they can stand it. A monk's work is hard; he works to free his heart in order to feel the loving-kindness that embraces all things. Seeing that all life rises and falls, is born and expires like the breath, he knows that nothing can belong to him, and thus he puts an end to suffering.

If we just practice with sincerity, the fruits of our practice will shine forth. Anyone with eyes can see. We do not have to advertise.

Restraint

The worldly way is outgoing, exuberant; the way of
the monk's life is restrained and controlled. Constantly work against the grain, against old habits; eat,
speak, and sleep little. If you are lazy, raise energy. If
you feel you cannot endure, raise patience. If you like
the body and feel attached to it, learn to see it as
unclean. Indulging your desires instead of opposing
them cannot even be considered the slow way, as a
month's rather than a day's journey. Instead, you will
simply never arrive. Work with your desires.

Virtue or following precepts, and concentration or
meditation are aids to the practice. They make the
mind calm and restrained. But outward restraint is
only a convention, a tool to help gain inner coolness.
You may keep your eyes cast down, but still your
mind may be distracted by whatever enters your field
of vision.

Perhaps you feel that this life is too difficult, that
you just cannot do it. But the more clearly you
understand the truth of things, the more incentive you
will have. Suppose you are walking home and step on
a large thorn that goes deep into your foot. In pain,
you feel you just cannot go on. Then a ferocious tiger
comes, and, afraid that it will "eat your head," you
forget about your foot, get up, and run all the way
home.

Constantly ask yourself, "Why am I ordained?" Let it be a spur. It is not for comfort and pleasure; these are much more easily had in lay life. On alms round, at any time, ask, "Why do I do what I do?" It should not be out of habit. Listening to the Dharma, are you hearing the teaching or mérely the sound? Maybe the words enter your ears, but you are thinking, "The sweet potatoes at breakfast were really delicious." Keep your mindfulness sharp. In activity around the monastery, the important point is intention; know what you are doing and know how you feel about it. Learn to know the mind that clings to ideas of purity and bad karma, burdens itself with doubt and excessive fear of wrongdoing. This too is attachment. Too much of this mind makes you afraid to sweep because you may kill ants, afraid to walk because you may harm the grass. New doubts constantly arise in regard to one's purity—if you keep following the anxiety, you only gain temporary relief. You must understand the process of doubt in order to put an end to it.

In our chanting, we say that we are the Buddha's servants. To be a servant means to give yourself completely to your master and rely on him for all your needs: food, clothing, shelter, guidance. We who wear the robes, an inheritance of the Buddha, should understand that all the requisites we receive from lay supporters come to us because of the virtue of the Buddha, not because of our own individual merit.

Know moderation in those requisites. Robes need not be of fine material, they are merely to protect the body. Alms-food is merely to sustain you. The Path constantly opposes defilement and habitual desire. When Sariputta was going for alms-food, he saw that greed said, "Give me a lot," so he said, "Give me a little." If defilement says, "Give it to me fast," our Path says, "Give it to me slowly." If attachment wants hot, soft food, then our Path asks for it hard and cold.

All our actions—wearing the robes, collecting alms-food—should be done mindfully, according to the precepts. The Dharma and discipline that the Buddha gave us are like a well-tended orchard. We do not have to worry about planting trees and caring for them; we do not have to be afraid that the fruit will be poisonous or unfit to eat. All of it is good for us.

Once inner coolness is attained, you still should not throw away the forms of monastic life. Be an example for those who come after; this is how the enlightened monks of old behaved.

Rules Are Tools

One should fear wrongdoings, sometimes even to the point of not being able to sleep. At first, cling to the rules, make them a burden. Afterwards, you can carry them lightly. But you must experience the heaviness first, just as before one can go beyond suffering, one must experience suffering. One who is conscientious is at first like a freshwater fish in salt water —trying to keep rules, his eyes will burn and sting. Whereas one who is indifferent and negligent will not be disturbed but will also never learn to see.

Working with the 227 precepts is essential to our monk's practice. We must follow the rules well. Yet the rules are endless. Keep in mind that rules are conventions or tools. There is no need to study all the expressions of Dharma or know all the rules. To cut a path through the forest, you need not cut down all the trees. Cutting just one row can take you to the other side.

The point of all practice is to lead you to freedom, to become one who knows the light all the time. The only way to reach an end in the practice of virtue is by making the mind pure.

Go Left, Go Right

A Western monk at Wat Ba Pong became frustrated by the difficulties of practice and the detailed and seemingly arbitrary rules of conduct the monks had to follow. He began to criticize other monks for sloppy practice and to doubt the wisdom of Achaan Chah's teaching. At one point, he went to Achaan Chah and complained, noting that even Achaan Chah himself was inconsistent and seemed often to contradict himself in an unenlightened way.

Achaan Chah just laughed and pointed out how much the monk was suffering by trying to judge others around him. Then he explained that his way of teaching is very simple: "It is as though I see people walking down a road I know well. To them the way may be unclear. I look up and see someone about to fall into a ditch on the right-hand side of the road, so I call out to him, 'Go left, go left!' Similarly, if I see another person about to fall into a ditch on the left, I call out, 'Go right, go right!' That is the extent of my teaching. Whatever extreme you get caught in, whatever you get attached to, I say, 'Let go of that too.' Let go on the left, let go on the right. Come back to the center, and you will arrive at the true Dharma."

Cures For Restlessness

Here are several ways to work with restlessness and an inability to concentrate:

Take very little food.

Do not talk with anyone.

After the meal, return to your hut, close the doors and windows, wrap yourself up in a lot of robes, and sit, no matter how you feel. In this way, you can face the restlessness directly. When feelings arise, question them and realize that they are only feelings.

As you go deeper into your practice, there will be times of great inner tension followed by release to the point of weeping. If you have not experienced this at least several times, you have not yet really practiced.

The "Deeper Meaning"
of a Chant

Each morning, the monks enter the eating hall after their alms round. Seated in two long rows with the last food distributed, they raise their hands in a palms-together gesture of respect while reciting the meal-time chants, ancient Pali blessings that date back to the time of the Buddha. Lay devotees who have come to offer food and participate in the meal sit by silently as the monks chant. Following this, in mindful stillness the monks begin their meal.

A Western visitor, new to the monastery and its traditions, asked Achaan Chah at the close of the recitation why the monks were chanting: "Is there some deep meaning to this ritual?" Achaan Chah smiled, "Yes, of course. It is important indeed for hungry monks to chant like this before the only meal of the day. The Pali recitation means *thank you*," he said, *"thank you very much."*

The Dharma of Menial Tasks

The practice here is not really that difficult, although some people do not like to do it. In the early days of Wat Ba Pong, there was no electricity, no large meeting hall or dining room. Now that we have them, we have to take care of them; conveniences always give rise to complications.

We each have various responsibilities in the monastery. Taking care of huts and bathrooms is important. Simple things are important, like cleaning the hall and washing bowls for elder monks, keeping huts and toilets clean. What is dirty, beginning with the body, we should recognize as such, but we should still keep them clean.

This is not crude or menial work; rather, you should understand that it is the most refined. Each activity done fully, mindfully, for its own sake, is an expression of our practice, of our Dharma.

Harmony With Others

One purpose of morality or virtue is harmony with our spiritual friends. This should be our aim, rather than just trying to fulfill our selfish desires. Knowing one's position and respecting one's seniors is an important part of our precepts.

For harmony with the group, we must give up pride and self-importance and attachment to fleeting pleasure. If you do not give up your likes and dislikes, you are not really making an effort. Not to let go means you seek peace where there is none. Discover this truth for yourself. No need to rely on a teacher outside—mind and body constantly preach to us. Listening to their sermon will remove all doubts.

People get caught in being the leader, the chief, or they get caught in being the student, the follower. Who can learn from all things without being the student? Who can teach all things without being the chief?

Make bowing a way to care for all the world around you. Bow with reverence and care. When returning to your cottage, put everything down and prostrate first thing. If you go out to sweep, prostrate first. Returning, prostrate. When you have to go to the bathroom, prostrate first, and do it again when you come back, saying in your mind: "Any misdeeds I have done through body, speech, and mind, may I be forgiven." Stay mindful always.

We monks are very fortunate. We have our dwelling place, good companions, lay support, and the teachings. All that is left is to practice.

Monks Don't Chatter

As for speaking little, saying just what is necessary, if someone asks, "Where are you going?" simply answer, "To get jackfruit wood." And if they ask further, "What are you going to do with the wood," just answer, "I'm going to dye my robes." Rather than, "Oh, I've just come from Umpur Muang, and I've heard there's some good jackfruit wood around, so I'll cut some and dye these robes, which I just finished sewing last week. Boy, what a job it's been! Say, what have you been doing this week?"

Ordained people should not be interested in chattering and socializing. Not that they should not speak at all, but they should only speak what is useful and necessary. In Achaan Mun's monastery, after the afternoon water hauling, sweeping, and bathing, no noise could be heard save the sound of the sandals of monks doing walking meditation. Once a week or so, the monks would gather for instruction and teaching, then go right back to their practice. The walking paths were well worn in those days, whereas today the only footprints to be found are often those of the village dogs.

Good meditation temples are increasingly hard to find. For most monks, Buddhism is a lot of study without real practice. Everywhere, there is more interest in cutting down forests and building new temples than in developing the mind. In earlier times, this was not the case—meditation teachers lived with nature and did not try to build anything. Now, offering buildings is the religious activity that most interests lay people. So be it. But we must know the purpose of having a monastery. The monk's own practice is 80 to 90 percent of his job, and the remainder of his time can be spent benefiting the public. Even then, those who teach the public should be ones who are in control of themselves and thus capable of helping others, not caught up with their own burdens.

The occasional talks the teacher gives are an opportunity to check out your state of mind and your practice. The points he teaches are important to work with. Can you see them in yourself? Are you practicing correctly or making certain mistakes? Do you have the right outlook? Nobody else can do this for you, you cannot end doubt by listening to others. You may assuage your uncertainty temporarily, but it will return and you will only have more questions. The only end to doubt is to put it to rest by yourself once and for all.

We must use the physical solitude of the forest to help develop mindfulness, not just for isolation and escape. How can we escape our mind and the three characteristics of conditioned phenomena? Really, suffering, impermanence and no self are everywhere. They are like the smell of excrement. Whether you have big piles or little piles, the smell is the same.

Opposing Lust

If the lay life were the most suitable for practice, the Buddha would not have had us become monks. Our bodies and minds are a gang of thieves and murderers, constantly pulling us toward the fires of greed, hatred, and delusion. In lay life, it is so much more difficult, with constant sense contact, as if someone were calling in welcoming tones from a house, "Oh, come here, please come here." and as you approached, they were to open the door and shoot you.

You can do ascetic practices, such as using worn-out unattractive things or doing the corpse meditation, looking at everyone you see, including yourself as a corpse or a skeleton. Yet these practices are not easy. As soon as you see a pretty young girl, you stop seeing corpses.

Body meditation is an example of opposition. We normally consider the body good and beautiful; the Path is to contemplate its impermanent and unpleasant aspects. When we are young and strong, not yet afflicted with serious illness, it is easy to think wrongly and act unskillfully. Death seems far away, one fears no one and nothing. If one does not meditate, a taste of illness and a realization of aging may be necessary to change one's outlook. Why wait for this? Just be as one who has died. Your desires have not yet died, it is true, but behave as if they had.

Sometimes it is necessary to go to extremes, such as living near dangerous beasts. If you know there are tigers and wild elephants about and fear for your life, you will not have time to think about sex. Or you can reduce your food or fast to temporarily reduce energy.

Some monks live in cemeteries and make death and decay their constant object of meditation. As a young monk, I liked to live with old men, asking them what it was like to get old, seeing them and realizing we all must go the same way. Constantly keeping death and decay in mind, dispassion and disappointment in the world of senses arise, leading to rapture and concentration. One sees things as they are and is free of them. Later, when meditation is firmly established, there are no difficulties. We are only driven by lust because meditation is not yet unshakable.

When we come to live in the forest as monks, we are no longer letting the defilements be content in their own way, so we find they kick at us quite hard. Patience and endurance are the only remedy. In fact, at times in our practice there is nothing else, only endurance. Yet of course it will all change.

People outside may call us mad to live in the forest like this, sitting like statues. But how do they live? They laugh, they cry, they are so caught up that, at times, they kill themselves or one another out of greed and hatred. Who are the mad ones?

Remember to keep in mind why we ordain. Anyone who comes to a practice like ours and does not taste enlightenment has wasted his time. Lay people with families, possessions, and responsibilities have attained it. One who is ordained should certainly be able to do the same.

Scenes Change, but the Mind Remains the Same

One would think that to relinquish all worldly life and take the robes and bowl of a forest monk should put an end to the concerns of possessions for a time. No longer the owner of car and stereo, books and wardrobe, the monk is free. But the movement of the attached mind is like a heavy flywheel that only slows down imperceptibly.

Therefore, some of the new Western monks soon became attached to their robes and bowl and monk's bag. Carefully, they dyed their robes just the right color or contrived ways to become owners of the newer, lightweight, stainless steel begging bowls. Concern and care for and even attachment to only two or three possessions can take a lot of time when one has little else to do but meditate.

Several of the Western monks who had been world travelers before ordination, extravagantly free in their dress and their lifestyle, soon found the surrender and conformity of the monastery oppressive and difficult. Heads are shaved just alike, robes are worn just alike, even the way to stand and to walk is prescribed. Bows to senior monks are performed just this way, the begging bowl is held in just such a manner. Even with the best intentions, a Westerner can find this surrender frustrating.

One particular monk had been not only a regular traveler, but as he described himself, a "costume" hippy, with bells and flowery embroidered capes, fancy hats, and long braids. The monastic conformity became so difficult after a few weeks that he was awakened in the middle of the night by a violent dream in which he had taken his golden robes and tie-died them red and green and had painted flowers and Tibetan designs over his black begging bowl.

Achaan Chah laughed when he heard this story the next morning. Then he asked about freedom in America. Did it have to do with hair style, with clothes? Perhaps, he reminded the monk as he sent him back to his meditation, there is a deeper meaning to freedom. His task was to discover that liberation beyond all circumstances and times.

For each who experiences this greed in the circumstances of renunciation and simplicity, it is a lesson illuminated as never before. The difficulty with possessiveness and desire is quite independent of external circumstances—it takes root in the heart and can take charge in any situation, with any quantity of goods. Until it is thoroughly understood and the lesson of relinquishment deeply learned, the new outer form becomes only another arena in which habits of greed play.

Achaan Chah is well aware of the power of the forest life to illuminate and at times exacerbate problems rooted in the mind/heart. His mastery is to use the ascetic discipline to allow monks to confront and work directly with their own problems of greed or judgment, hatred or ignorance. And his teachings always turn the monks back to their own minds, the source and the root of all trouble.

Where Can You Run To?

People come and ordain as monks, but when they face themselves here, they are not at peace. Then they think of disrobing, running away. But where else can they go to find peace?

Know what is good and bad, whether traveling or living in one place. You cannot find peace on a mountain or in a cave; you can travel to the site of Buddha's enlightenment without coming any closer to the truth.

Doubting is natural at first: Why do we chant? Why do we sleep so little? Why do we sit with our eyes closed? Questions like these arise when we start practicing. We must see all the causes of suffering— this is the true Dharma, the Four Noble Truths, not any specific method of meditation. We must observe what is actually happening. If we observe things, we will see that they are impermanent and empty, and a little wisdom arises. Yet we still find doubt and boredom returning because we do not really know reality yet, we do not see it clearly. This is not a negative sign. It is all part of what we must work with, our own mental states, our own hearts and minds.

Looking for the Buddha

Achaan Chah has been unusually tolerant of the comings and goings of his Western disciples. Traditionally, a new forest monk will spend at least five rains retreats with his first teacher before beginning his ascetic wanderings. Achaan Chah stresses discipline as a major part of his practice—working precisely and carefully with the monks' rules and learning to surrender to the monastic style and to the way of the community. But somehow Western monks, like favored children, have been allowed more than the traditional space to travel in order to visit other teachers. Usually when someone does leave, there is no fuss and not much memory. Life in the Dharma is immediate, full, and complete. Achaan Chah has said that from where he sits, "Nobody comes and nobody goes."

After only a year and a half of practice at Wat Ba Pong, one American asked and received permission to travel and study with other Thai and Burmese teachers. A year or two later, he returned full of tales of his travels, of many months of extraordinary and intensive practice and of a number of remarkable experiences. After completing his usual prostrations, he was greeted as if he had never left. At the end of the morning Dharma discussion and business with monks and visitors, Achaan Chah finally turned to him and asked if he had found any new or better Dharma out-side the forest monastery. No, he had learned many new things in his practice, but actually, they were to be found at Wat Ba Pong as well. The Dharma is always right here for anyone to see, to practice. "Ah yes," Achaan Chah laughed, "I could have told you that before you left, but you wouldn't have understood."

Then the Western monk went to the cottage of Achaan Sumedho, the senior Western disciple of Achaan Chah, and told all his stories and adventures, his new understandings and great insights into prac-tice. Sumedho listened in silence and prepared after-noon tea from the roots of certain forest plants. When the stories were completed and the insights recounted, Sumedho smiled and said, "Ah, how wonderful. Something else to let go of." Only that.

Yet the Westerners kept coming and going, all to learn these lessons for themselves. At times, Achaan Chah would bless their travels; often, though, he would tease.

An English monk, vacillating in his search for the perfect life, the perfect teacher, had come and gone, ordained and disrobed, several times. "This monk," Achaan Chah finally chided, "has dog droppings in his monk's bag, and he thinks every place smells bad."

Another English monk who had come and gone— from the monastery, to Europe, to a job, to a mar-riage engagement, to monkhood several times—was seated one day at Achaan Chah's cottage. "What this monk is looking for," Achaan Chah declared to the assembly, "is a turtle with a mustache. How far do you think he will have to travel to find it?"

Out of frustration, another Western monk went to

Achaan Chah asking permission to leave. Practice and surrender to the monastic life were hard, and this monk began to find fault with all that surrounded him. "The other monks talk too much. Why do we have to chant? I want more time alone to meditate. The senior monks don't teach newcomers very well, and even you," he said to Achaan Chah in desperation, "even you don't seem so enlightened. You're always changing—sometimes you're strict, sometimes you don't seem to care. How do I know you're enlightened?"

Achaan Chah laughed heartily at this, which both amused and irritated the young monk. "It's a good thing I don't appear to be enlightened to you," he said, "because if I fit your model of enlightenment, your ideal of how an enlightened person should act, you would still be caught looking for the Buddha outside yourself. He's not out there—he's in your own heart."

The monk bowed and returned to his cottage to look for the real Buddha.

Rely on Oneself

Sitting cross-legged on a hard stone temple floor is natural to villagers who have grown up in a culture without furniture. But to one newly arrived Western novice, gawky and inflexible, it was a hard way to begin the daily hours of meditation and chanting. Thus it was with some relief the novice discovered that by arriving early to meditation, he could sit next to the stone pillars at the front of the hall and, once all the monks had closed their eyes to practice, he could gently lean on the pillar and meditate in Western-style comfort.

After a week of this practice, Achaan Chah rang the bell to end the sitting and start the evening Dharma talk. "Tonight," he began, looking directly at the new monk, "we will talk about how practicing the Dharma means to support oneself, to rely on oneself, to not have to lean on things outside of oneself." The other monks in the hall tittered. The Westerner, a bit embarrassed, sat up unusually straight for the rest of the lecture. From that point on his resolve grew firm, and he learned how to sit straight on any floor under any conditions.

Keep the Teaching Simple

A large piece of wild forest land was offered Achaan Chah by nearby villagers to start a monastery. A wealthy lay supporter heard of this and offered to build a magnificent hall and temple on top of a small mountain in the forest. Other lay supporters gathered together, and a design was drawn for the largest Dharma hall in several provinces. Huts for monks were built in caves around the mountain, and a road was laboriously cut through the woods. Construction commenced on the Dharma hall: concrete foundation, tall pillars, platform for a giant bronze Buddha. As work proceeded, new designs were added. Complex discussions between lay sponsors and the builders ensued. Just how fancy should the roof be? Should we modify the design to make it better in this way? In that way? How about hollow pillars and a huge rainwater tank underneath? Everyone had good ideas, but they were all very costly.

The culmination of all these discussions was a long meeting with Achaan Chah. Construction experts, lay sponsors, all presented the different design options, the costs, the time for building. Finally the wealthy lay supporter spoke up with her ideas and questions. "Tell us, Achaan, which of these designs to follow. The frugal one? The costly one? How shall we proceed?"

Achaan Chah laughed. "When you do good, there are good results." That was all he would say.

The finished Dharma hall was magnificent.

Learning to Teach

Makkha Puja is an important Buddhist holiday celebrating the coming together of 1,250 enlightened disciples in the Buddha's presence. At this meeting, he told them to "wander forth" spreading the Dharma "for the good, the benefit, and the awakening" of beings everywhere.

To celebrate this holiday, Achaan Chah and his many hundred monks sit up all night in meditation with the village lay supporters. In a typical year the great hall is filled with perhaps a thousand villagers. They sit for an hour, then Achaan Chah or one of his chief disciples, who are all abbots of their own monasteries, gives an inspiring Dharma talk. Again they sit for an hour, alternating sitting and talks all night long.

One of the earliest Western students of Achaan Chah was seated among the group of new monks feeling the inspiration and joy and difficulty of this night-long celebration and practice. At the completion of one hour of sitting in the middle of the night, Achaan Chah announced to the villagers that they would now hear a talk in their native Lao language by the Western monk. The monk was as surprised as the villagers, but having no chance to prepare or to get nervous, he sat in front of the assembly and spoke of the inspiration that had brought him to ordain and of

134

the new understandings of the Dharma he had gleaned from practice. After this experience, he was rarely ever nervous about speaking before a group.

Achaan Chah later explained that Dharma teaching must flow unprepared from the heart and from inner experience. "Sit, close the eyes, and step out of the way," he said. "Let the Dharma speak itself."

On another occasion, Achaan Chah asked Achaan Sumedho, his senior Western monk, to speak. Sumedho talked for a half hour. "Speak a half hour more," said Achaan Chah. A half hour later, Achaan Chah said "Speak more still." Sumedho continued, becoming increasingly boring. Many of the listeners started to doze. "Surrender to speaking," Achaan Chah cajoled. "Just do it." After struggling on for several hours, Sumedho had learned to bore his listeners thoroughly and was never again afraid of their judgments when he talked.

Achaan Chah asked a monk who was leaving if he was planning to teach when he got back to the West. No, he had no particular plans to teach Dharma, he replied, although if someone asked, he would do his best to explain how to practice.

"Very good," Achaan Chah said, "it is beneficial to speak about the Dharma to those who inquire. And when you explain it," he went on, "why not call it Christianity. They won't understand in the West if you say anything about Buddha.

"I speak of God to Christians, yet I have not read their books. I find God in the heart. Do you think God is Santa Claus, who comes once a year with gifts for children? God is Dharma, the truth; the one who sees this sees all things. And yet God is nothing special—just this.

"What we are really teaching is how to be free from suffering, how to be loving and wise and filled with compassion. This teaching is the Dharma, anywhere in any language. So call it Christianity. Then it will be easier for some of them to understand."

Achaan Chah had this advice for an aspiring Dharma teacher:

"Don't let them scare you. Be firm and direct. Be clear about your own shortcomings, and acknowledge your limits. Work with love and compassion, and when people are beyond your ability to help, develop equanimity. Sometimes teaching is hard work. Teachers become garbage cans for people's frustrations and problems. The more people you teach, the bigger the garbage disposal problem. Don't worry. Teaching is a wonderful way to practice Dharma. The Dharma can help all those who genuinely apply it in their lives. Those who teach grow in patience and understanding."

Achaan Chah encourages his students to share what they learn. "When you have learned the truth, you will be able to help others, sometimes with words but mostly through your being. As for conversing about Dharma, I am not so adept at it. Whoever wants to know me should live with me. If you stay for a long time, you will see. I myself wandered as a forest monk for many years. I did not teach—I practiced and listened to what the masters said. This is important advice: when you listen, really listen. I do not know what else to say."

He had said enough to last us a long time.

What Is The Best Kind Of Meditation?

Achaan Chah is surrounded by visitors most of the day—students, farmers, politicians, generals, pilgrims, devotees. They ask for blessings, seek advice, question him, praise him, challenge him, blame him, and bring him a thousand problems to solve. He teaches this constant stream of people without rest. One day he was heard to remark how he had learned as much Dharma from receiving them as from any other practice.

A Wonderful Meal

Some Students asked Achaan Chah why he so rarely talks about Nirvana but teaches instead about wisdom in daily life. Other teachers speak so often of attaining Nirvana, of its special bliss and its importance in their practice.

Achaan Chah answered that some people will savor a good meal and then go on to praise its merits to everyone they meet. Others will eat and savor the same meal but, once through, will feel no need to go around telling others of a meal already eaten.

Achaan Chah's Cottage

Achaan Chah says he does not dream any more. He sleeps only a few hours a night, upstairs in a small one-room cottage. Underneath this cottage, which is on wooden pillars in Thai fashion, is an open floor where he receives visitors.

Often these visitors bring him gifts, not just food or robes but also exquisite ancient statues and carefully made folk art depicting Buddhist themes. One Western monk, a collector and appreciator of Asian art, was excited by the possibility of seeing such lovely objects when he was assigned to help with the daily cleaning of Achaan Chah's cottage. He went upstairs, unlocked the door, and found only a bare bed and a mosquito net. He discovered that Achaan Chah gives these gifts away as fast as he gets them. He does not cling to anything.

Holy Ceremonies and Hot Days

Since the time of the Buddha himself, monks have been called upon to perform ceremonies, to make blessings, or to bring comfort in times of difficulties in the lives of lay disciples. The Buddha himself is said to have employed the tradition of soothing the hearts of his disciples with holy water and blessings.

Because the life of study and ceremony has taken the place of genuine practice for most monks in Thailand, Achaan Chah usually jokes about these ceremonies as diversions on the Path. Nevertheless, he will also use ceremonies when they are helpful. One very hot afternoon he had been invited to town to give a Dharma talk and a blessing ceremony for some devoted lay students. After the preliminary chanting and Dharma discourse, Achaan Chah proceeded to chant over a brass bowl of water connected by a string through the hands of the eight monks accompanying him (remnants of the ancient Hindu sacred thread) to a large image of the Buddha in meditation. The chanting over the water was completed with an offering of candles and incense, and Achaan Chah stood up with a palm leaf to sprinkle this water as a blessing on the house and on those who came to hear the Dharma.

One young Western monk in the party was growing impatient in the heat and yet more impatient with the ceremony. "Why do you bother with such obviously useless ceremonies like this when they have nothing to do with practice?" he whispered to Achaan Chah. "Perhaps because," the teacher whispered back, "it's a hot day and all these people want a cool shower."

The Real Magic

The villagers and other disciples around Wat Ba Pong tell many tales of Achaan Chah's powers. They say he can make his body manifest in several places at once and some claim to have seen his double. They tell of his great healing powers, of his cures of the sick, or they speak of his power to know the minds of others, of his clairvoyance and penetrating samadhi.

Achaan Chah laughs at these stories, at the unenlightened concern for, the misguided awe of such powers. "There is only one real magic," he says, "the magic of the Dharma, the teachings that can liberate the mind and put an end to suffering. Any other magic is like the illusion of a card trick—it distracts us from the real game, our relation to human life, to birth and death, and to freedom. At Wat Ba Pong," he says, "we only teach the real magic."

On another occasion he told the monks: "Of course, if one reaches samadhi, it can be used for other purposes—cultivating psychic powers, or making holy water, blessings, charms, and spells. If you reach this level, such things can be done. Practicing like that is intoxicating, like drinking good liquor. But over here is where the Path is, the way the Buddha passed. Here samadhi is used as a foundation for vipassana, contemplation, and need not be very great. Just observe what is arising, continue observing cause and effect, continue contemplating. In this way, we use the focused mind to contemplate sights, sounds, smells, tastes, bodily contacts, and mental objects." It is in our very senses that the whole Dharma of liberation can be found.

Practice for the Householder

You have often asked about the path of the householder. Household life is both hard and easy—hard to do, easy to understand. It is as if you were to come complaining to me with a red-hot coal in your hand, and I were to tell you to simply drop it. "No, I won't," you say. "I want it to be cold." Either you must drop it, or you must learn to be very patient.

"How can I drop it?" you ask. Can you just drop your family? Drop it in your heart. Let go of your inner attachment. You are like a bird that has laid eggs; you have a responsibility to sit with and hatch them. Otherwise, they will become rotten.

You may want the members of your family to appreciate you, to understand why you act in certain ways, yet they may not. Their attitude may be intolerant, closed-minded. If the father is a thief and the son disapproves, is he a bad child? Explain things as well as you can, make an honest effort, then let go. If you have a pain and go to the doctor, but he and all his medicines cannot cure it, what can you do but let it go?

If you think in terms of *my* family, *my* practice, this kind of self-centered view is just another cause of suffering. Do not think of finding happiness, either living with others or living alone—just live with the

Dharma. Buddhism helps to work out problems, but we must practice and develop wisdom first. You do not just throw rice into a potful of water and immediately have boiled rice. You have to build the fire, bring the water to a boil, and let the rice cook long enough. With wisdom, problems can eventually be solved by taking into account the karma of beings. Understanding family life, you can really learn about karma, about cause and effect, and can begin to take care of your action in the future.

Practicing in a group, in a monastery, or at a retreat is not so hard; you are too embarrassed to miss sittings with others. But when you go home, you find it difficult; you say that you are lazy or unable to find time. You give away your personal power, projecting it onto others, onto situations or teachers outside yourself. Just wake up! You create your own world. Do you want to practice or not?

Just as we monks must strive with our precepts and ascetic practices, developing the discipline that leads to freedom, so you lay people must do likewise. As you practice in your homes, you should endeavor to refine the basic precepts. Strive to put body and speech in order. Make real effort, practice continuously. As for concentrating the mind, do not give up because you have tried it once or twice and are not at peace. Why should it not take a long time? How long have you let your mind wander as it wished without doing anything to control it? How long have you allowed it to lead you around by the nose? Is it any wonder that a month or two is not enough to still it?

Of course, the mind is hard to train. When a horse is really stubborn, do not feed it for a while—it will come around. When it starts to follow the right course, feed it a little. The beauty of our way of life is that the mind can be trained. With our own right effort, we can come to wisdom.

To live the lay life and practice Dharma, one must be in the world but remain above it. Virtue, beginning with the five basic precepts, is all important, parent to all good things. It is the basis for removing wrong from the mind, removing the cause of distress and agitation. Make virtue really firm. Then practice your formal meditation when the opportunity presents itself. Sometimes the meditation will be good, sometimes not. Do not worry about it, just continue. If doubts arise, just realize that they, like everything else in the mind, are impermanent.

As you continue, concentration will arise. Use it to develop wisdom. See like and dislike arising from sense contact and do not attach to them. Do not be anxious for results or quick progress. An infant first crawls, then learns to walk, then to run. Just be firm in your virtue and keep practicing.

PART VI
Questions for the Teacher

One of the most delightful ways to receive instruction from Achaan Chah is to sit at his cottage and listen *as* he answers questions for the monks of the monastery and the constant stream of lay visitors. It is here that one can see the universality of this way of practice, for although on some days he might discuss only the rice crop with a local farmer, most of the questions one hears are the same from Asians and Westerners alike. They ask about doubts and fears, the ways to calm the heart, the possibilities and struggles in living a virtuous and meditative life.

One or two hundred or more European and American students have found their way to the rural forest of Thailand to practice at Wat Ba Pong and its branch monasteries over the years. They include seekers and travelers, physicians and Peace Corps volunteers, old and young. Some have come to ordain for good and make the monk's path their way of life. Others stay for shorter periods of training and then return to the West to integrate and apply the way of mindfulness to their household life.

Some of the questions which follow were asked during the 1970 rains retreat by monks, both Western and Thai. Others came from a more recent session during a visit by Western lay students and Dharma teachers to Wat Ba Pong. If you listen carefully to the answers to these questions, you will find each points to a way of practice and freedom you can use in your own life. Each contains the seeds of the Dharma of liberation, and each points you back to the source of true insight and understanding—your own heart and mind.

Questions and Answers

One part of these questions, answers, and discussions with Achaan Chah was recorded during the visit of a group of Western disciples and Dharma teachers to Wat Ba Pong. Included also are parts of the questions and answers from *Living Buddhist Masters*,* gathered at an earlier period during the 1970 rains retreat at Wat Ba Pong monastery.

Q: *How should we start our practice? Must we begin practice with strong faith?*
A: Many people start out with little faith and little understanding. This is quite natural. We all must start where we are. What matters is that those who practice must be willing to look into their own mind, their own circumstances, to learn about themselves directly. Then faith and understanding will mature in their hearts.

Q: *I'm trying very hard in my practice, but I don't seem to be getting anywhere.*
A: Don't try to get anywhere in practice. The very desire to be free or to be enlightened will be the desire

---

*Jack Kornfield, *Living Buddhist Masters* (Boulder, Colo.: Shambhala, 1983). Reprinted by permission of the publisher.

that prevents your freedom. You can try as hard as you wish, practice ardently night and day, but if you still have the desire to achieve, you will never find peace. The energy from this desire will cause doubt and restlessness. No matter how long or how hard you practice, wisdom will not arise from desire. Simply let go. Watch the mind and body mindfully, but don't try to achieve anything. Otherwise, when you are beginning to practice meditation and your heart starts to quiet down, you will immediately think, "Oh, am I near the first stage yet? How much further do I have to go?" In that instant, you will lose everything. It is best just to observe how practice naturally develops.

You have to pay attention without any concept of levels, simply and directly to what's happening in your heart or mind. The more you watch, the more clearly you'll see. If you learn to pay attention totally, then you don't have to worry about what stage you have attained; just continue in the right direction, and things will unfold for you naturally.

How can I speak of the essence of practice? To walk forward is not correct, to back up is not correct, and to stand still is not correct. There is no way to measure or categorize liberation.

Q: *But aren't we seeking deeper concentration in practice?*
A: In sitting practice, if your heart becomes quiet and concentrated, that's an important tool to use. But you have to be careful not to be stuck in tranquillity. If you're sitting just to get concentrated so you can feel happy and pleasant, you're wasting your time. The practice is to sit and let your heart become still and

concentrated and then to use that concentration to examine the nature of the mind and body. Otherwise, if you simply make the heart / mind quiet, it will be peaceful and free of defilement only as long as you sit. This is like using a stone to cover a garbage pit; when you take away the stone, the pit is still infested and full of garbage. The question is not how long or short you sit. You must use your concentration not to temporarily get lost in bliss but to deeply examine the nature of the mind and body. This is what actually frees you.

Examining the mind and body most directly does not involve the use of thought. There are two levels of examination. One is thoughtful and discursive, keeping you trapped in a superficial perception of experience. The other is a silent, concentrated, inner listening. Only when the heart is concentrated and still can real wisdom naturally arise. In the beginning, wisdom is a very soft voice, a tender young plant just beginning to spring up out of the ground. If you don't understand this, you may think too much about it and trample it underfoot. But if you feel it silently, then in that space, you can begin to sense the basic nature of your body and mental process. It is this seeing that leads you to learn about change, about emptiness, and about selflessness of body and mind.

Q: *But if we are not seeking anything, then what is the Dharma?*
A: Everywhere you look is the Dharma; constructing a building, walking down the road, sitting in the bathroom, or here in the meditation hall, all of this is Dharma. When you understand correctly, there is nothing in the world that is not Dharma.

151

But you must understand. Happiness and unhappiness, pleasure and pain are always with us. When you understand their nature, the Buddha and the Dharma are right there. When you can see clearly, each moment of experience is the Dharma. But most people react blindly to anything pleasant, "Oh, I like this, I want more," and to anything unpleasant, "Go away, I don't like this, I don't want any more." If, instead, you can allow yourself to open fully to the nature of each experience in the simplest way, you will become one with the Buddha.

It's so simple and direct once you understand. When pleasant things arise, understand that they're empty. When unpleasant things arise, understand that they're not you, not yours; they pass away. If you don't relate to phenomena as being you or see yourself as their owner, the mind comes into balance. This balance is the correct path, the correct teaching of the Buddha which leads to liberation. Often people get so excited—"Can I attain this or that level of samadhi?" or "What powers can I develop?" They completely skip over the Buddha's teaching to some other realm that's not really useful. The Buddha is to be found in the simplest things in front of you, if you're willing to look. And the essence of this balance is the nongrasping mind.

When you begin to practice, it's important to have a proper sense of direction. Instead of just trying to imagine which way to go and wandering around in circles, you must consult a map or someone who's been there before in order to establish a sense of the path. The way to liberation first taught by the Buddha was the Middle Path lying between the extremes of indulgence in desire and self-mortification. The mind must be open to all experience without losing its balance and falling into these extremes. This allows you to see things without reacting and grabbing or pushing away.

When you understand this balance, then the path becomes clear. As you grow in understanding, when things come that are pleasant, you will realize that they won't last, that they're empty, that they offer you no security. Unpleasant things will also present no problem because you will see that they won't last either, that they're equally empty. Finally, as you travel further along the path, you will come to see that nothing in the world has any essential value. There's nothing to hold on to. Everything is like an old banana peel or a coconut husk—you have no use for it, no fascination with it. When you see that things in the world are like banana peels that have no great value for you, then you're free to walk in the world without being bothered or hurt in any way. This is the path that brings you to freedom.

Q: *Do you recommend that students do long, intensive, silent retreats?*
A: It's largely an individual matter. You must learn to practice in all kinds of situations, both in the marketplace and when you're really alone. Yet to start where it's quiet is helpful; that's one reason we live in the forest. In the beginning you do things slowly, working to become mindful. After a time you can learn to be mindful in any situation.

Some people have asked about doing six months or a year of silent, intensive practice. For this there can be no rule; it has to be determined individually. It's like the ox carts that the villagers use around here. If the driver is going to carry a load to some town, he has to assess the strength of the cart, the wheels, and the oxen. Can they make it, or can't they? In the same way, the teacher and the student must be sensitive both to possibilities and to limitations. Is the student ready for this sort of practice? Is this the right time? Be sensitive and sensible; know and respect your own limits. This is also wisdom.

Buddha talked about two styles of practice: liberation through wisdom and liberation through concentration. People whose style is liberation through wisdom hear the Dharma and immediately begin to understand it. Since the entire teaching is simply to let go of things, to let things be, they begin the practice of letting go in a very natural way, without a great deal of effort or concentration. This simple practice can take them eventually to that place beyond self where there is no more letting go and no one to hold on.

Some people, on the other hand, depending on their background, need a lot more concentration. They have to sit and practice in a very disciplined way over a long period of time. For them, this concentration, if it is used properly, becomes the basis for deep, penetrating insight. Once the mind is concentrated, it's like having finished high school—you can now go on to college and study any number of things. Once samadhi is strong, you can enter the different planes of absorption, or you can experience all the levels of insight, depending on how you choose to use it.

In either case, liberation through wisdom and liberation through concentration must arrive at the same freedom in practice. Any of the tools of our practice applied without attachment can bring us to liberation. Even the precepts—whether the five precepts for householders, the ten precepts for novices, or the 227 precepts for monks—can be used in the same way. Because these are disciplines that require mindfulness and surrender, there is no limit to their usefulness. For example, if you keep refining just the basic precept of being honest, applying it to your outer actions and inner contemplation, it has no limit. Like any other Dharma tool, it can set you free.

Q: *Is it useful to do loving kindness meditation as a separate part of practice?*
A: Repeating words of loving kindness can be useful, but this is a rather elementary practice. When you have really looked into your own mind and done the essential Buddhist practice correctly, you will understand that true love appears. When you let go of self and other, then there is a deep, natural development that is different from the child's play of repeating the formula, "May all beings be happy; may all beings not suffer."

Q: *Where should we go to study the Dharma?*
A: If you look for the Dharma, you will find that it has nothing to do with the forests, the mountains, or the caves—it exists only in the heart. The language of the Dharma isn't English or Thai or Sanskrit. It has its own language, which is the same for all people—the language of experience. There is a great difference between concepts and direct experience. Whoever puts a finger into a glass of hot water will have the same experience of hot, but it is called by many words in different languages. Similarly, whoever looks deeply into the heart will have the same experience, no matter

what his or her nationality or culture or language. If in your heart you come to that taste of Dharma, you become one with others, like joining a big family.

Q: *Then is Buddhism much different from other religions?*
A: It is the business of genuine religions, including Buddhism, to bring people to the happiness that comes from clearly and honestly seeing how things are. Whenever any religion or system or practice accomplishes this, you can call that Buddhism, if you like.

In the Christian religion, for example, one of the most important holidays is Christmas. A group of the Western monks decided last year to make a special day of Christmas, with a ceremony of gift-giving and merit-making. Various other disciples of mine questioned this, saying, "If they're ordained as Buddhists, how can they celebrate Christmas? Isn't this a Christian holiday?"

In my Dharma talk, I explained how all people in the world are fundamentally the same. Calling them Europeans, Americans, or Thais just indicates where they were born or the color of their hair, but they all have basically the same kind of minds and bodies; all belong to the same family of people being born, growing old, and dying. When you understand this, differences become unimportant. Similarly, if Christmas is an occasion where people make a particular effort to do what is good and kind and helpful to others in some way, that's important and wonderful, no matter what system you use to describe it.

So I told the villagers, "Today we'll call this Chrisbuddhamas. As long as people are practicing properly, they're practicing Christ-Buddhism, and things are fine." I teach this way to enable people to let go of their attachments to various concepts and to see what is happening in a straightforward and natural way. Anything that inspires us to see what is true and do what is good is proper practice. You may call it anything you like.

Q: *Do you think that the minds of Asians and Westerners are different?*
A: Basically, there is no difference. Outer customs and language may appear different, but the human mind has natural characteristics that are the same for all people. Greed and hatred are the same in an Eastern or a Western mind. Suffering and the cessation of suffering are the same for all people.

Q: *Is it advisable to read a lot or to study the scriptures as a part of practice?*
A: The Dharma of the Buddha is not found in books. If you want to really see for yourself what the Buddha was talking about, you don't need to bother with books. Watch your own mind. Examine to see how feelings and thoughts come and go. Don't be attached to anything, just be mindful of whatever there is to see. This is the way to the truths of the Buddha. Be natural. Everything you do in your life here is a chance to practice. It is all Dharma. When you do your chores, try to be mindful. If you are emptying a spittoon or cleaning a toilet, don't feel you are doing it as a favor for anyone else. There is Dharma in emptying spittoons. Don't feel you are practicing only when sitting still, cross-legged. Some of you have complained that there is not enough time to meditate. Is there enough time to breathe? This is your meditation: mindfulness, naturalness, in whatever you do.

Q: *Why don't we have daily interviews with the teacher?*
A: If you have questions, you're welcome to come and ask them any time. But we don't need daily interviews here. If I answer your every little question, you will never understand the process of doubt in your own mind. It is essential that you learn to examine yourself, to interview yourself. Listen carefully to the lecture every few days, then use this teaching to compare with your own practice. Is it the same? Is it different? Do you have doubts? Who is it that doubts? Only through self-examination can you understand.

Q: *What can I do about doubts? Some days I'm plagued with doubts about the practice or my own progress or the teacher.*
A: Doubting is natural. Everyone starts with doubts. You can learn a great deal from them. What is important is that you don't identify with your doubts. That is, don't get caught up in them, letting your mind spin in endless circles. Instead, watch the whole process of doubting, of wondering. See who it is that doubts. See how doubts come and go. Then you will no longer be victimized by your doubts. You will step outside of them, and your mind will be quiet. You can see how all things come and go. Just let go of what you're attached to. Let go of your doubts and simply watch. This is how to end doubting.

Q: *What about other methods of practice? These days, there seem to be so many teachers and so many different systems of meditation that it's confusing.*
A: It's like going into town. One can approach from the north, from the southeast, from many roads. Often these systems just differ outwardly. Whether

you walk one way or another, fast or slow, if you are mindful, it's all the same. There's one essential point that all good practice must eventually come to—not clinging. In the end, you must let go of all meditation systems. Nor can you cling to the teacher. If a system leads to relinquishment, to not clinging, then it is correct practice.

You may wish to travel, to visit other teachers and try other systems. Some of you have already done so. This is a natural desire. You will find out that a thousand questions asked and knowledge of many systems will not bring you to the truth. Eventually you will get bored. You will see that only by stopping and examining your own heart can you find out what the Buddha talked about. No need to go searching outside yourself. Eventually, you must return to face your own true nature. Right where you are is where you can understand the Dharma.

Q: *Often it seems that many monks here are not practicing. They look sloppy or unmindful, and this disturbs me.*
A: Seeing other monks behaving badly, you get annoyed and suffer unnecessarily, thinking, "He is not as strict as I am. They are not serious meditators like us. They are not good monks."

Trying to get everyone to act as you wish them to act will only make you suffer. No one can practice for you, nor can you practice for anyone else. Watching other people will not help your practice; watching other people will not develop wisdom. It is a great defilement on your part.

Don't make comparisons. Don't discriminate. Discrimination is dangerous, like a road with a very sharp curve. If we think others are worse than, better than, or the same as we are, we spin off the road. If we discriminate, we will only suffer. It is not for you to judge whether others' discipline is bad or they are good monks. The discipline of monks is a tool to use for your own meditation, not a weapon for criticizing or finding fault.

Let go of your opinions and watch yourself. This is our Dharma. If you're annoyed, watch the annoyance in your own mind. Just be mindful of your own actions; simply examine yourself and your feelings. Then you will understand. This is the way to practice.

Q: *I have been extremely careful to practice sense restraint. I always keep my eyes lowered and am mindful of every little action I do. When eating, for example, I take a long time and try to see each step— chewing, tasting, swallowing, and so on—and I take each step deliberately and carefully. Am I practicing properly?*

A: Sense restraint is proper practice. We should be mindful of it throughout the day. But don't overdo it. Walk, eat, and act naturally, and then develop natural mindfulness of what is going on within yourself. To force your meditation or force yourself into awkward patterns is another form of craving. Patience and endurance are necessary. If you act naturally and are mindful, wisdom will come naturally.

Q: *Then what is your advice to new practitioners?*
A: The same as for old practitioners! Keep at it.

Q: *I can observe anger and work with greed, but how does one observe delusion?*
A: You're riding a horse and asking "Where's the horse?" Pay attention.

Q: *What about sleep? How much should I sleep?*
A: Don't ask me, I can't tell you. What's important, though, is that you watch and know yourself. If you try to go with too little sleep, the body will feel uncomfortable, and mindfulness will be difficult to sustain. Too much sleep, on the other hand, leads to a dull or restless mind. Find the natural balance for yourself. Carefully watch the mind and body, and keep track of sleep needs until you find the optimum. To wake up and then roll over for a snooze is defilement. Establish mindfulness as soon as your eyes open.

As for sleepiness, there are many ways to overcome it. If you are sitting in the dark, move to a lighted place. Open your eyes. Get up and wash or slap your face, or take a bath. If you are sleepy, change postures. Walk a lot. Walk backwards. The fear of running into things will keep you awake. If this fails, stand still, clear the mind, and imagine it's broad daylight. Or sit on the edge of a high cliff or deep well. You won't dare sleep! If nothing works, then just go to sleep. Lie down carefully, and try to be aware until the moment you fall asleep. Then as soon as you awaken, get right up.

Q: *How about eating? What is the proper amount to eat?*
A: Eating is the same as sleeping. You must know yourself. Food must be consumed to meet bodily needs. Look at your food as medicine. Are you eating so much that you feel sleepy after the meal and are getting fatter every day? Try to eat less. Examine your own body and mind, and as soon as five more spoonfuls will make you full, stop and take water until just properly full. Go and sit. Watch your sleepiness and

hunger. You must learn to balance your eating. As your practice deepens, you will naturally feel more energetic and eat less. But you must adjust yourself.

Q: *Is it necessary to sit for very long periods of time?*
A: No, sitting for hours on end is not necessary. Some people think that the longer you can sit, the wiser you must be. I have seen chickens sit on their nests for days on end. Wisdom comes from being mindful in all postures. Your practice should begin as soon as you awaken in the morning and should continue until you fall asleep. Don't be concerned about how long you can sit. What's important is only that you keep watchful, whether you're walking or sitting or going to the bathroom.

Each person has his own natural pace. Some of you will die at age fifty, some at age sixty-five, and some at age ninety. So, too, your practices will not be identical. Don't think or worry about this. Try to be mindful, and let things take their natural course. Then your mind will become still in any surroundings, like a clear forest pool. All kinds of wonderful, rare animals will come to drink at the pool, and you will clearly see the nature of all things. You will see many strange and wonderful things come and go, but you will be still. This is the happiness of the Buddha.

Q: *I still have many thoughts, and my mind wanders a lot, even though I'm trying to be mindful.*
A: Don't worry about this. Just try to keep your mind in the present. Whatever arises in the mind, just watch it and let go of it. Don't even wish to be rid of thoughts. Then the mind will return to its natural state. No discriminating between good and bad, hot and cold, fast and slow. No me and no you, no self

162

at all—just what there is. When you walk there is no need to do anything special. Simply walk and see what is there. No need to cling to isolation or seclusion. Wherever you are, know yourself by being natural and watching. If doubts arise, watch them come and go. It's very simple. Hold on to nothing.

It's as though you are walking down a road. Periodically you will run into obstacles. When you meet defilements, just see them and overcome them by letting them go. Don't think about the obstacles you've already passed; don't worry about those you have not yet seen. Stick to the present. Don't be concerned about the length of the road or the destination. Everything is changing. Whatever you pass, don't cling to it. Eventually the mind will reach its natural balance where practice is automatic. All things will come and go of themselves.

Q: *What about specific hindrances which are difficult? For example, how can we overcome lust in our practice? Sometimes I feel as if I'm a slave to my sexual desire.*
A: Lust should be balanced by contemplation of loathsomeness. Attachment to bodily form is one extreme, and one should keep the opposite in mind. Examine the body as a corpse and see the process of decay, or think of the parts of the body, such as lungs, spleen, fat, feces, and so forth. Remembering these and visualizing the loathsome aspects of the body will free you from lust.

Q: *How about anger? What should I do when I feel anger arising?*
A: You can just let go of it, or else learn to use loving-kindness. When angry states of mind arise

strongly, balance them by developing feelings of loving-kindness. If someone does something bad or gets angry, don't get angry yourself. If you do you are being more ignorant than they. Be wise. Keep compassion in mind, for that person is suffering. Fill your mind with loving-kindness as if he were a dear brother. Concentrate on the feeling of loving-kindness as a meditation subject. Spread it to all beings in the world. Only through loving-kindness is hatred overcome.

Q: *Why must we do so much bowing?*
A: Bowing is a very important outward form of the practice that should be done correctly. Bring the forehead all the way to the floor. Have elbows near the knees about three inches apart. Bow slowly, mindful of your body. It is a good remedy for our conceit. We should bow often. When you bow three times, you can keep in mind the qualities of the Buddha, the Dharma, and the Sangha, that is, the qualities of purity, radiance, and peace. We use the outward form to train ourselves, to harmonize body and mind. Don't make the mistake of watching how others bow. If young novices are sloppy or the aged monks appear unmindful, this is not for you to judge. People can be difficult to train. Some learn fast, but others learn slowly. Judging others will only increase your pride. Watch yourself instead. Bow often; get rid of your pride.

Those who have really become harmonious with the Dharma get far beyond the outward form. Because they have gone beyond selfishness, everything they do is a way of bowing—walking, they bow; eating, they bow; defecating, they bow.

Q: *What is the biggest problem for your new disciples?*

A: Opinions. Views and ideas about all things, about themselves, about practice, about the teachings of the Buddha. Many of those who come here have a high rank in the community. They are wealthy merchants, college graduates, teachers, government officials. Their minds are filled with opinions about things, and they are too clever to listen to others. Those who are too clever leave after a short time; they never learn. You must get rid of your cleverness. A cup filled with dirty, stale water is useless. Only after the old water is thrown out can the cup become useful. You must empty your minds of opinions; then you will see. Our practice goes beyond cleverness and stupidity. If you think, "I am clever, I am wealthy, I am important, I understand all about Buddhism," you cover up the truth of *anatta,* or non-self. All you will see is self, I, mine. But Buddhism is letting go of self—voidness, emptiness, Nirvana. If you think yourself better than others, you will only suffer.

Q: *Are defilements such as greed or anger merely illusory, or are they real?*

A: They are both. The defilements we call lust or greed, anger and delusion, are just outward names and appearances, just as we call a bowl large, small, or pretty. If we want a big bowl, we call this one small. We create such concepts because of our craving. Craving causes us to discriminate, while the truth is merely what is. Look at it this way. Are you a man? Yes? This is the appearance of things. But you are really only a combination of elements or a group of changing aggregates. If the mind is free it doesn't discriminate. No big and small, no you and me, nothing. We say *anatta*, or not-self, but really, in the end, there is neither *atta* nor *anatta*.

Q: *Could you explain a little more about karma?*
A: Karma is action. Karma is clinging. Body, speech, and mind all make karma when we cling. We create habits that can make us suffer in the future. This is the fruit of our attachment, of our past defilement.

When we were young, our parents used to get angry and discipline us because they wanted to help us. We got upset when parents and teachers criticized us, but later, we could see why. That is like karma. Suppose you were a thief before you became a monk. You stole, made others, including your parents, unhappy. Now you are a monk, but when you remember how you made others unhappy, you feel badly and suffer even today. Or if you did some act of kindness in the past and remember it today, you will be happy, and this happy state of mind is the result of past karma.

Remember, not only body but also speech and mental action can make conditions for future results. All things are conditioned by cause, both long-term and moment-to-moment. But you need not bother to think about past, present, or future; merely watch the body and mind now. You can figure out your karma for yourself if you watch your mind. Practice and you will see clearly. After long practice you will know.

Make sure, however, that you leave others to their own karma. Don't cling to or watch others. If I take poison, I suffer; no need for you to share it with me. Take the good that your teacher offers. Then your mind will become peaceful like the mind of your teacher.

166

Q: *Sometimes it seems that since becoming a monk, I have increased my hardships and suffering.*
A: I know that some of you have had a background of material comfort and outward freedom. By comparison, you now live an austere existence. In the practice, I often make you sit and wait for long hours, and food and climate are different from your home. But everyone must endure some of this—the suffering that leads to the end of suffering—in order to learn.

All my disciples are like my children. I have only loving-kindness and their welfare in mind. If I appear to make you suffer, it is for your own good. When you get angry and feel sorry for yourself, it is a great opportunity to understand the mind. The Buddha called defilements our teachers. People with little education and worldly knowledge can practice easily, but I know some of you are well educated and very knowledgeable. It is as if you Westerners have a very large house to clean. When you have cleaned the house, you will have a big living space. You must be patient. Patience and endurance are essential to our practice.

When I was a young monk, I did not have it as hard as you. I knew the language and was eating my native food. Even so, some days I despaired. I wanted to disrobe or even commit suicide. This kind of suffering comes from wrong views. When you have seen the truth, though, you are freed from views and opinions. Everything becomes peaceful.

Q: *I have been developing very peaceful states of mind from meditation. What should I do now?*
A: This is good. Make the mind peaceful, concentrated, and use this concentration to examine the mind and body. When the heart and mind are not peace-

ful, you should also watch. Then you will know true peace. Why? Because you will see impermanence. Even peace must be seen as impermanent. If you are attached to peaceful states of mind, you will suffer when you do not have them. Give up everything, even peace.

Q: *Did I hear you say that you're afraid of very diligent disciples?*
A: Yes, that's right. I'm afraid that they're too serious. They try too hard, without wisdom, pushing themselves into unnecessary suffering. Some of you have determined to become enlightened. You grit your teeth and struggle all the time. You're just trying too hard. You should just see that people are all the same—they don't know the nature of things. All formations, mind and body, are impermanent. Simply watch and don't cling.

Q: *I have been meditating for many years. My mind is open and peaceful in almost all circumstances. Now I would like to try to backtrack and practice high states of concentration or mind absorption.*
A: Such practices are beneficial mental exercise. If you have wisdom, you will not get hung up on concentrated states of mind. In the same way, wanting to sit for long periods is fine for training, but practice is really separate from any posture. Directly looking at the mind is wisdom. When you have examined and understood the mind, you have the wisdom to know the limitations of concentration or books. If you have practiced and have understood not clinging, you can then return to the books as to a sweet dessert, and they can also help you to teach others. Or you can return to practicing absorption-concentration with the wisdom to know not to hold on to anything.

Q: *Please say more about how to share the Dharma with others.*

A: To act in ways that are kind and wholesome is the most basic way to further the teaching of Buddha. To do what is good, to help other people, to work with charity and morality, brings good results, brings a cool and happy mind for yourself and others.

To teach other people is a beautiful and important responsibility that one should accept with a full heart. The way to do it properly is to understand that in teaching others you must always be teaching yourself. You have to take care of your own practice and your own purity. It's not enough to simply tell others what's correct. You must work with what you teach in your own heart, being unwaveringly honest with yourself and with others. Acknowledge what is pure and what is not. The essence of the Buddha's teaching is to learn to see things truthfully, fully and clearly. Seeing the truth in itself brings freedom.

Q: *Would you review some of the main points of our discussion?*

A: You must examine yourself. Know who you are. Know your body and mind by simply watching. In sitting, in sleeping, in eating, know your limits. Use wisdom. The practice is not to try to achieve anything. Just be mindful of what is. Our whole meditation is to look directly at the heart/mind. You will see suffering, its cause, and its end. But you must have much patience and endurance. Gradually you will learn. The Buddha taught his disciples to stay with their teacher for at least five years.

Don't practice too strictly. Don't get caught up with outward form. Simply be natural and watch that. Our monk's discipline and monastic rules are very important. They create a simple and harmonious environ-

169

ment. Use them well. But remember, the essence of the monk's discipline is watching intention, examining the heart. You must have wisdom.

Watching others is bad practice. Don't discriminate. Would you get upset at a small tree in the forest for not being tall and straight like some of the others? Don't judge other people. There are all varieties—no need to carry the burden of wishing to change them all.

You must learn the value of giving and of devotion. Be patient; practice morality; live simply and naturally; watch the mind. This practice will lead you to unselfishness and peace.

PART VII
Realization

*It is a wonderful discovery to see that the enlighten-
ment and joy described in the ancient Buddhist texts
still exist today. We see it in Achaan Chah who
stresses its timeless nature and speaks to us as a living
example. He urges us to understand and realize
freedom in our own hearts through right practice and
true understanding.*

*And, indeed, this is possible. People today, as
through the centuries, are discovering enlightenment
through the path of insight and mindfulness, not only
Achaan Chah but his students as well, and those of
many other Buddhist teachers. It is here to discover.
Its essence is no farther than our own bodies and
mind. Achaan Chah puts it very directly: Lay it all
down, all grasping and judging, don't try to be
anything. Then in the stillness you can let yourself see
through the whole illusion of self. We don't own any
of it. When we are inwardly silent and awake, we will
come to this realization spontaneously and freely. No
permanent self. No one inside. Nothing. Just the play
of the senses.*

*This realization brings freedom, vitality, joy. The
sense of life's burdens drops, together with the sense
of self. What is left is reflected in these pages, clarity
and openness of heart, a wise and free spirit.*

As Achaan Chah says, why not give it a try?

Not-Self

When one does not understand death, life can be very confusing. If our body really belonged to us, it would obey our commands. If we say, "Don't get old," or "I forbid you to get sick," does it obey us? No, it takes no notice. We only rent this house, not own it. If we think it belongs to us, we will suffer when we have to leave it. But in reality, there is no such thing as a permanent self, nothing solid or unchanging that we can hold on to.

Buddha made a distinction between ultimate truth and conventional truth. The idea of a self is merely a concept, a convention—American, Thai, teacher, student, all are conventions. Ultimately no one exists, only earth, fire, water, and air—elements that have combined temporarily. We call the body a person, my self, but ultimately there is no me, there is only *anatta*, not-self. To understand not-self, you have to meditate. If you only intellectualize, your head will explode. Once you understand not-self in your heart, the burden of life will be lifted. Your family life, your work, everything will be much easier. When you see beyond self, you no longer cling to happiness, and when you no longer cling to happiness, you can begin to be truly happy.

Short and Straight

A devout, elderly village lady from a nearby province came on a pilgrimage to Wat Ba Pong. She told Achaan Chah she could stay only a short time, as she had to return to take care of her great grandchildren, and since she was an old lady, she asked if he could please give her a brief Dharma talk.

He replied with great force, "Hey, listen. There's no one here, just this. No owner, no one to be old, to be young, to be good or bad, weak or strong. Just this, that's all; various elements of nature playing themselves out, all empty. No one born and no one to die. Those who speak of death are speaking the language of ignorant children. In the language of the heart, of Dharma, there's no such thing.

"When we carry a burden, it's heavy. When there's no one to carry it, there's not a problem in the world. Do not look for good or bad or for anything at all. Do not be anything. There's nothing more; just this."

Underground Water

The Dharma belongs to no one; it has no owner. It arises in the world when a world manifests, yet stands alone as the truth. It is always here, unmoving, limitless, for all who seek it. It is like water underground—whoever digs a well finds it. Yet whether or not you dig, it is always here, underlying all things.

In our search for the Dharma, we search too far, we overreach, overlooking the essence. The Dharma is not out there, to be gained by a long voyage viewed through a telescope. It is right here, nearest to us, our true essence, our true self, no self. When we see this essence, there are no problems, no troubles. Good, bad, pleasure, pain, light, dark, self, other, are empty phenomena. If we come to know this essence, we die to our old sense of self and become truly free.

We practice to give up, not to attain. But before we can give up mind and body, we must know their true nature. Then detachment naturally arises.

Nothing is me or mine, all is impermanent. But why can't we say nirvana is mine? Because those who realize nirvana do not have thoughts of me or mine. If they did, they could not realize nirvana. Although they know the sweetness of honey, they do not think, "I am tasting the sweetness of honey."

The Dharma Path is to keep walking forward. But the true Dharma has no going forward, no going backward, and no standing still.

The Joy of the Buddha

If all is impermanent, unsatisfactory, and selfless, then what is the point of existence? One man watches a river flow by. If he does not wish it to flow, to change ceaselessly in accord with its nature, he will suffer great pain. Another man understands that the nature of the river is to change constantly, regardless of his likes and dislikes, and therefore he does not suffer. To know existence as this flow, empty of lasting pleasure, void of self, *is* to find that which is stable anc̄ free of suffering, to find true peace in the world.

"Then," some people may ask, "what is the meaning of life? Why are we born?" I cannot tell you. Why do you eat? You eat so that you do not have to eat anymore. You are born so that you will not have to be born again.

To speak about the true nature of things, their voidness or emptiness, is difficult. Having heard the teachings, one must develop the means to understand.

Why do we practice? If there is no why, then we are at peace. Sorrow cannot follow the one who practices like this.

The five aggregates are murderers. Being attached to body, we will be attached to mind, and vice versa. We must cease to believe our minds. Use the precepts and calming of the heart to develop restraint and constant mindfulness. Then you will see happiness and displeasure arising and not follow either, realizing that all states are impermanent, unsatisfactory, and empty. Learn to be still. In this stillness will come the true joy of the Buddha.

Picking Up Mangoes

When you have wisdom, contact with sense objects, whether good or bad, pleasant or painful, is like standing at the bottom of a mango tree and collecting the fruit while another person climbs up and shakes it down for us. We get to choose between the good and rotten mangoes, and we do not waste our strength because we do not have to climb up the tree.

What does this mean? All the sense objects that come to us are bringing us knowledge. We do not need to embellish them. The eight worldly winds—gain and loss, fame and disrepute, praise and blame, pain and pleasure—come of their own. If your heart has developed tranquillity and wisdom, you can enjoy picking and choosing. What others may call good or bad, here or there, happiness or suffering, is all to your profit, because someone else has climbed up to shake the mangoes down, and you have nothing to fear.

The eight worldly winds are like mangoes falling down to you. Use your concentration and tranquillity to contemplate, to collect. Knowing which fruits are good and which are rotten is called wisdom, vipassana. You do not make it up or create it. If there is wisdom, insight arises naturally. Although I call it wisdom, you do not have to give it a name.

The Timeless Buddha

The original heart/mind shines like pure, clear water
with the sweetest taste. But if the heart is pure, is our
practice over? No, we must not cling even to this
purity. We must go beyond all duality, all concepts,
all bad, all good, all pure, all impure. We must go
beyond self and no self, beyond birth and death. To
see a self to be reborn is the real trouble of the world.
True purity is limitless, untouchable, beyond all op-
posites and all creation.

We take refuge in Buddha, Dharma, and Sangha.
This is the heritage of every Buddha that appears in
the world. What is this Buddha? When we see with
the eye of wisdom, we know that the Buddha is
timeless, unborn, unrelated to any body, any history,
any image. Buddha is the ground of all being, the
realization of the truth of the unmoving mind.

So the Buddha was not enlightened in India. In fact
he was never enlightened, was never born, and never
died. This timeless Buddha is our true home, our
abiding place. When we take refuge in the Buddha,
Dharma, and Sangha, all things in the world are free
for us. They become our teacher, proclaiming the one
true nature of life.

Yes, I Speak Zen

A visiting Zen student asked Achaan Chah, "How old are you? Do you live here all year round?"

"I live nowhere," he replied. "There is no place you can find me. I have no age. To have age, you must exist, and to think you exist is already a problem. Don't make problems; then the world has none either. Don't make a self. There's nothing more to say."

Perhaps the Zen student glimpsed that the heart of vipassana is no different from the heart of Zen.

The Unstruck Gong

Living in the world and practicing meditation, you
will seem to others like a gong that has not been
struck and is not producing any sound. They will consider you useless, mad, defeated; but actually, just the
opposite is true.

Truth is hidden in untruth, permanence is hidden in
impermanence.

Nothing Special

People have asked about my own practice. How do I prepare my mind for meditation? There is nothing special. I just keep it where it always is. They ask, "Then are you an arhat (one who has reached a high stage of spiritual progress)?" Do I know? I am like a tree, full of leaves, blossoms, and fruit. Birds come to eat and to nest. Yet the tree does not know itself. It follows its nature; it is as it is.

Inside You is Nothing, Nothing at All

In my third year as a monk, I had doubts about the nature of samadhi and wisdom. Really desiring to experience samadhi, I strove ceaselessly in my practice. As I sat in meditation, I would try to figure out the process, and therefore my mind was especially distracted. When I did nothing in particular and was not meditating, I was fine. But when I determined to concentrate my mind, it would become extremely agitated.

"What's going on?" I wondered. "Why should it be like this?" After a while, I realized that concentration is like breathing. If you determine to force your breaths to be deep or shallow, fast or slow, breathing becomes difficult. But when you are just walking along, not aware of your inhalation and exhalation, breathing is natural and smooth. In the same way, any attempt to force yourself to become tranquil is just an expression of attachment and desire and will prevent your attention from settling down.

As time went by, I continued to practice with great faith and growing understanding. Gradually I began to see the natural process of meditation. Since my desires were clearly an obstacle, I practiced more openly, investigating the elements of mind as they occurred. I sat and watched, sat and watched, over and over again.

One day, much later in my practice, I was walking in meditation sometime after 11 P.M. My thoughts were almost absent. I was staying at a forest monastery and could hear a festival going on in the village in the distance. After I became tired from walking meditation, I went to my hut. As I sat down, I felt that I could not get into the cross-legged posture fast enough. My mind naturally wanted to enter into deep concentration. It just happened on its own. I thought to myself, "Why is it like this?" When I sat, I was truly tranquil; my mind was firm and concentrated. Not that I did not hear the sound of singing coming from the village, but I could make myself not hear it as well.

With the mind one-pointed, when I turned it toward sounds, I heard; when I did not, it was quiet. If sounds came, I would look at the one who was aware, who was separate from sounds, and contemplate, "If this isn't it, what else could it be?" I could see my mind and its object standing apart, like this bowl and kettle here. The mind and the sounds were not connected at all. I kept examining in this way, and then I understood. I saw what held subject and object together, and when the connection was broken, true peace emerged.

On that occasion, my mind was not interested in anything else. If I were to have stopped practicing, I could have done so at my ease. When a monk stops practicing, he is supposed to consider: "Am I lazy? Am I tired? Am I restless?" No, there was no laziness or tiredness or restlessness in my mind, only completeness and sufficiency in every way.

When I stopped for a rest, it was only the sitting that stopped. My mind remained the same, unmoved. As I lay down, at that moment my mind was tranquil as before. As my head hit the pillow, there was a turning inward in the mind. I did not know where it was turning, but it turned within, like an electric current being switched on, and my body exploded with loud noises. The awareness was as refined as seemed possible. Passing that point, the mind went in further. Inside was nothing, nothing at all; nothing went in there, nothing could reach. The awareness stopped inside for awhile and then came out. Not that I made it come out—no, I was merely an observer, the one who was aware.

When I came out of this condition, I returned to my normal state of mind, and the question arose, "What was that?" The answer came, "These things are just what they are; there's no need to doubt them." Just this much said, and my mind could accept.

After it had stopped for awhile, the mind turned inward again. I did not turn it, it turned itself. When it had gone in, it reached its limit as before. This second time, my body broke into fine pieces, and the mind went further in, silent, unreachable. When it had gone in and stayed for as long as it wished, it came out again, and I returned to normal. During this time, the mind was self-acting. I did not try to make it come and go in any particular way. I only made myself aware and observed. I did not doubt. I just continued to sit and contemplate.

The third time the mind went in, the whole world broke apart: the earth, grass, trees, mountains, people, all was just space. Nothing was left. When the mind had gone in and abided as it wished, had stayed for as long as it could, the mind withdrew, and returned to normal. I do not know how it abided; such things are difficult to see and to speak about. There is nothing to compare it with.

Of these three instances, who could say what had occurred? Who could know? What could I call it? What I have spoken about here is all a matter of the nature of mind. It is not necessary to speak of the categories of mental factors and consciousness. With strong faith I went about practice, ready to stake my life, and when I emerged from this experience the whole world had changed. All knowledge and understanding had been transformed. Someone seeing me might have thought I was mad. In fact, a person without strong mindfulness might well have gone mad, because nothing in the world was as before. But it was really just I who had changed, and yet still I was the same person. When everyone would be thinking one way, I would be thinking another; when they would speak one way, I would speak another. I was no longer running with the rest of humankind.

When my mind reached the peak of its power, it was basically a matter of mental energy, of the energy of concentration. On the occasion I just described, the experience was based on the energy of samadhi. When samadhi reaches this level, vipassana flows effortlessly.

If you practice like this, you do not have to search very far. Friend, why don't you give it a try?

There is a boat you can take to the other shore. Why not jump in? Or do you prefer the ooze and the slime? I could paddle away any time, but I am waiting for you.

In Ending

In ending, I hope that you will continue your journeys and practice with much wisdom. Use the understanding that you have already developed to persevere in practice. This can become the ground for your growth, for the deepening of yet greater understanding and love. You can deepen your practice in many ways. If you are timid in practice, then work with your mind so that you can overcome that. With the proper effort and with time, understanding will unfold by itself. But in all cases, use your own natural wisdom. What we have spoken of is what I feel is helpful to you. If you really do it, you can come to the end of all doubt. You come to where you have no more questions, to that place of silence, to the place in which there is oneness with the Buddha, with the Dharma, with the universe. And only you can do that.

From now on it's up to you.

Glossary

Abhidharma. Buddhist psychology, which teaches a detailed analysis of the components and processes of mind and body.

Bhikkhu. A fully ordained Buddhist monk who has taken 227 training vows of renunciation and simplicity.

Body, speech, and mind. The three spheres of action that can be observed and trained in Buddhist practice.

Concentration. The mental factor of one-pointedness of mind, steadiness of mind on an object. Also those meditation practices which develop strong concentration and tranquillity by focusing on a steady object.

Consciousness. The knowing faculty of mind, that aspect of mind which knows the sense objects arising and passing away at the six sense doors.

Defilements. The mental factors of greed, hatred, and delusion, and mental states which arise with these as their root.

Delusion. The mental factor of cloudiness of mind which does not allow objects to be seen clearly in the light of impermanence, suffering, and emptiness.

Dependent Origination. The twelve-link chain of becoming which causes the cycling of birth and death. Each link provides the condition for the arising of the next. Thus ignorance conditions the arising of formative tendencies, which conditions the arising of consciousness, which is followed by the links of mind and matter, the six sense bases, contact, sense impression, feeling, craving, clinging, the process of becoming, rebirth, and finally the last link of old age, sorrow, suffering, and death.

Dharma. The universal law or truth, the teachings of the Buddha about this law, and the elements which make up the process of experience.

Eightfold Path. The Buddhist path to purification and liberation—right understanding, right thought, right speech, right action, right livelihood, right effort, right mindfulness, and right concentration.

Elements. Usually refers to the four great elements of solidity (earth), cohesion (water), temperature (fire), and movement or vibration (air). Also used to refer to secondary physical elements and at times to elements of mind.

Elements of the mind. Includes the four mental processes of consciousness, feelings, perception, and volition or reaction to experience. May be further described as 52 basic mental qualities such as joy, greed, fear, calm, and so forth, which arise with consciousness and the object of experience.

Emptiness. Emptiness of self or soul; refers to the basic understanding that there is no one, no self to whom all experience is happening, and that what we are is simply a changing process.

Feeling. The mental factor of pleasant, unpleasant, or neutral feeling that arises in relation to an object.

Five aggregates. The five interlinked processes which make up a human being. They are the physical body, feelings, perceptions, volitions, and consciousness.

Four foundations of mindfulness. The four fields for awareness that are our whole experience and where we must pay attention to develop insight. They are: (1) the body and material elements, (2) feelings—pleasant, unpleasant, and neutral, (3) consciousness, and (4) all mental factors, all objects of mind, such as thoughts, emotions, greed, and love.

Four Noble Truths. The most basic teaching of the Buddha: (1) the truth of suffering, (2) the truth of the cause of suffering—clinging and desire, (3) the truth of the end of suffering, and (4) the path to the end of suffering—the Eightfold Path.

Greed. The mental factor which causes the mind to grasp or stick to an object or experience.

Hatred. The mental factor of aversion, which causes the mind to dislike or strike against an object or experience.

Ignorance. That basic force which does not see clearly the nature of the world and is the root cause of grasping and of our desire systems.

Impermanence. The basic truth that all phenomena which have the nature to arise must pass away.

Insight meditation (vipassana). Seeing clearly; meditation that focuses on the basic nature of the mind-body process to understand its true characteristics.

Karma. The law of cause and effect which describes the relationship between events in the realm of mind and of matter.

Matter. The physical world made of the four basic elements.

Mental factors. In the five aggregates, this refers to volition and the various other mental factors which arise in relation to consciousness and an object.

Mental formations or thought constructions. The conditioned process of volition, categorization, and reaction which determines our relationship to experience.

Mind. Includes consciousness plus the various mental factors which color consciousness.

Mindfulness. That quality of mind which notices what is happening in the present moment with no clinging, aversion, or delusion.

Nirvana. That state of total coolness beyond the movement of the mind-body process. Also refers to liberation from all greed, hatred, and delusion in the mind of an enlightened being.

Noble Ones. Those who have attained at least the first stage or glimpse of enlightenment and whose understanding and faith is unshakable.

Perception. The mental factor which perceives or recognizes objects.

Practice. The ongoing training of the heart and mind in generosity, virtue, calm, and wisdom.

Precepts. The Buddhist training rules for developing virtue. Laypersons keep five (refraining from killing, stealing, lying, sexual misconduct, and intoxicants which cause heedlessness); nuns and novices keep ten; and monks keep 227.

Samsara. The world of conditioned phenomena, of the elements of mind and matter, all of which are subject to constant change.

Sense bases. The six subjective-objective sense bases are: (1) the eye and visible objects, (2) the ear and sounds, (3) the nose and odors, (4) the tongue and tastes, (5) the body and bodily impressions, and (6) the mind and mind-objects.

Sitting. To sit in meditation, focusing the attention on some aspect of one's physical or mental states.

Suffering. The basic unsatisfactory, insecure nature of all transient phenomena.

Three Gems (the Three Jewels or Refuges). The Buddha, the Dharma (the Law and his teachings of it), and the Sangha (the community of monks and practitioners).

Virtue. Initially refers to following certain moral precepts; more deeply refers to acting in the world without greed, hatred, or delusion.

About the Translators

Jack Kornfield is co-founder of the Insight Meditation Society
(Barre, Massachusetts, 01005), a major teaching center for
Vipassana meditation in the West. He has taught at the Naropa
Institute, Esalen Institute, and other centers worldwide. After
beginning Asian and Buddhist studies at Dartmouth College in
1963, he spent six years in Asia, studying and practicing both as a
layman and a monk in several of the great monasteries and
meditation centers of the Theravada Buddhist tradition. The
Venerable Achaan Chah was one of his main teachers, although
he has also studied under several other masters during the past
eighteen years. Upon return from Asia he completed a Ph.D.
degree in clinical psychology. His published works include *A
Guide to Meditation Temples of Thailand* (W.F.B. publications),
Living Buddhist Masters (Prajna Press, Shambhala Publications),
and a forthcoming book with Joseph Goldstein, *Dharma Talks*
(Shambhala Publications).

Paul Breiter was trained and ordained as a Theravadin Buddhist
monk under the guidance of the Venerable Achaan Chah. He
became one of Achaan Chah's earliest Western disciples, living as
a monk for seven years. His study and practice allowed him to
become fluent in the Thai and Lao languages. He is translator of a
volume of the *Vinayamukka*, an important text on the monastic
life (published in English by the Royal Monkut Dharma University). He also studied extensively in the Zen and Vajrayana traditions and was ordained as a Zen priest by master Kobun Chino
Sensei. He continues his Buddhist practice under the guidance of
the Venerable Lama Gonpo, Rinpoche, a senior Lama of the
Tibetan Nyingmapa lineage.